WILLIAM F. MAAG LIBRARY
YOUNGSTOWN STATE UNIVERSITY

Best Poems of 1976

Best Poems of 1976
Borestone Mountain Poetry Awards 1977

A Compilation of Original Poetry
Published in Magazines of the
English-Speaking World in 1976

Volume 29

Pacific Books, Publishers, Palo Alto, California
1977

Copyright © 1977 by Borestone Mountain Poetry Awards.
All rights reserved.

International Standard Book Number 0-87015-227-0.
Library of Congress Catalog Card Number 49-49262.
Printed and bound in the United States of America.

PACIFIC BOOKS, PUBLISHERS
P.O. Box 558, Palo Alto, California 94302

FOREWORD

Best Poems of 1976 presents the Borestone Mountain Poetry Awards' twenty-ninth annual selections of poems from magazines of the English-speaking world issued in 1976. The selections are poems of not more than one hundred lines first printed in 1976. No reprints or translations are considered, and poems are not solicited or accepted directly from the poets. The reading staff and editors, working independently of one another, select from assigned magazines the poems they believe to be the most outstanding. In this way some three hundred poems are selected by the end of the year, and approximately one hundred and fifty magazines covered in the English-speaking world.

When the year's selections are complete, copies of the poems are sent to the editors serving as judges with the names of the authors and magazines deleted, as there is no intention of recognizing established names in preference to newcomers or apportioning selections between magazines and countries. The judges score their top seventy-five individual preferences and forward the results to the office of the Managing Editor, where a tabulation of the scores determines the final selections. The three highest scores are the winners of the year's cash awards. Because of the anonymity preserved during the selection process, the final results may include more than one poem by a poet and a number of poems from the same periodical.

"The Retrieval System" by Maxine Kumin received the first award of $300; "Saint Francis and the Sow" by Galway Kinnell won the second award of $200; and Dan Masterson's "For a Child Going Blind" received the third award of $100.

This is the final volume to be published in this series. After publication of Volume 29, Borestone Mountain Poetry Awards and the literary foundation will be closed. Most of the editors have served from the beginning years of the project and are considered founding members. They have given countless hours to the project. Because the time has arrived when new editors would have to take over the awards, and possibly turn them in new directions, we have concluded that it is best to bow out with twenty-nine published volumes, which have presented more than 2,200 poems by approximately 1,000 contemporary poets.

Borestone Mountain Poetry Awards, founded thirty-one years ago, has been supported by a not-for-profit literary foundation by the same name. The purpose of the awards was to preserve in book form each year some of the poems of merit that otherwise might be lost among countless magazine pages. The editors thank all those who have encouraged and supported Borestone Mountain Poetry Awards.

The editors also gratefully acknowledge permission to reprint these selected poems from the magazines, publishers, and authors owning the copyrights. Listed in the Contents are the magazines and issues in 1976 from which the selections were made. At the time the selections were completed in April 1977, some poems were scheduled for reprinting in collections of the poets. These subsequent printings and other recognitions are recorded under Acknowledgments and Notes.

THE EDITORS

HOWARD SERGEANT
British Commonwealth Magazines (except Canada)

WADDELL AUSTIN
Managing Editor

HILDEGARDE FLANNER

FRANCES MINTURN HOWARD

GEMMA D'AURIA

GARY MIRANDA

ACKNOWLEDGMENTS AND NOTES

"Knossus" by Loren Eiseley was selected from its first printing in the September 1976 issue of *Poetry*. The poem has been included in his collection of poems, *Another Kind of Autumn*, published by Charles Scribner's Sons in 1977.

"A Woman with Her Plants Talking" by Carol Frost also appeared in her chapbook, *The Salt Lesson*, published by the Graywolf Press, Port Townsend, Washington, copyright © 1977 by Carol Frost.

"Excavations" by Don Gordon is a selection from the January 1976 issue of *Harper's*, copyright © 1976 by Harper's Magazine.

"As I Came I Saw a Wood" by Ted Hughes is copyrighted 1976 by Ted Hughes.

"Two Horses" by Ted Hughes, copyright 1976 by Ted Hughes, was published in the English edition of *Season Songs* by Faber and Faber, London.

"Place Names" by Kate Jennings is reprinted from *The American Scholar*, Vol. 45, No. 3, Summer 1976, copyright © 1976 by the United Chapters of Phi Beta Kappa, by permission of the publishers.

"The Retrieval System" by Maxine Kumin was copyrighted © 1976 by the Atlantic Monthly Company, Boston, Massachusetts, and is reprinted with their permission.

"The Home Place" by Greg Kuzma is reprinted from *The American Scholar*, Vol. 45, No. 4, Autumn 1976, copyright © 1976 by the United Chapters of Phi Beta Kappa, by permission of the publishers.

"Vision" by Edward Lowbury, originally selected from the August 1976 issue of *New Statesman*, was included in the P.E.N. anthology, *New Poems 1976-77*, edited by Howard Sergeant.

"Sharks at the New York Aquarium" by Charles Martin, selected from the January 1976 issue of *Poetry*, is included in *Room for Error* by Charles Martin, copyright 1978 by the University of Georgia Press, to be published in January 1978.

"For a Child Going Blind" by Dan Masterson will also appear in his volume of poems to be printed in the spring of 1978 by the University of Illinois Press, Urbana, Illinois.

"... In Many Bodies" by Hugh McKinley also appeared in his collection of poems, *The Transformation of Faust and Other Poems*, published by Golgonooza Press, Ipswich, England.

"Immersion" by Jarold Ramsey was copyrighted © 1976 by the Atlantic Monthly Company, Boston, Massachusetts, and reprinted with their permission.

"The Ancestors and What They Left" by Ira Sadoff will be included in his collection of poems, *Palm Reading in Winter*, to be published by Houghton Mifflin Company in February 1978.

"A Man and His Watch" by Robert B. Shaw is to be included in a collection of his poems, *Comforting the Wilderness*, scheduled for publication in the fall of 1977. The copyright to the poem has been assigned by *Poetry* to Robert B. Shaw.

"Back River Winter" by Dave Smith, selected from the original printing in Vol. XXIX, No. 1 of *The Hudson Review*, appeared in his collection of poems, *Cumberland Station*, published by the University of Illinois Press, copyright © 1976 by Dave Smith.

"Some Marvelous Quarry" by Radcliffe Squires is reprinted by permission from *The Hudson Review*, Vol. XXIX, No. 2 (Summer 1976), copyright © 1976 by The Hudson Review, Inc.

"Elegy for Agatha Christie" by Pamela Stewart is included in her book, *The St. Vlas Elegies*, published by the L'Epervier Press, Fort Collins, Colorado, in July 1977.

"Sweater" by Mary Swander was selected from the original printing in the Winter 1976 issue of *The Ohio Review*. The poem has appeared in a chapbook of her poems, *Needlepoint*, published by the Smokeroot Press, Department of English, University of Montana, Missoula, Montana.

"Her Dream" by David Wagoner was selected from the January 6, 1976 issue of *The New Yorker*. The poem was included in *Collected Poems, 1956-1976*, by David Wagoner and is reprinted by permission of Indiana University Press, copyright © 1976 by Indiana University Press.

"Midsummer, England" by Derek Walcott is reprinted with the permission of Farrar, Straus & Giroux, Inc., from *Sea Grapes* by Derek Walcott, copyright © 1971, 1973, 1974, 1975, 1976 by Derek Walcott. The poem was selected from the February 9, 1976 issue of *The New Yorker*.

"From the Other Country" by Andrew Waterman was selected from the Aug./Sept. 1976 issue of *The London Magazine*. The poem was included in a collection of his poems of the same title, *From the Other Country*, published by Carcanet New Press of Manchester, England in 1977, copyright © 1977 by Andrew Waterman.

Tom Wayman has been assigned the copyright on his poem, "Grandmother," printed in the *American Review*, Vol. 24 (April 1976).

Miller Williams has been assigned the copyright on his poem, "Why God Permits Evil — for Answer To This Question of Interest to Many — Write Bible Answers Dept. E-7," printed in the Summer 1976 issue of *The Southern Review*.

"The Aftermath" and "Blight on Elm" by Daryl Hine are to be included in a collection of his poems to be published by Atheneum Publishers, New York, in 1978.

"St. Vincent's" by W. S. Merwin was selected from the December 13, 1976 issue of *The New Yorker*. The poem was included in his book, *The Compass Flower*, published in 1977 by Atheneum Publishers, New York, copyright © 1977 by W. S. Merwin.

The poems "Saint Francis and the Sow" (page 3), "For a Child Going Blind" (page 4), "Song" (page 29), "Burden" (page 30), "Blight on Elm" (page 48), "Henry Manley, Living Alone, Keeps Time" (page 58), "Splitting Wood at Six Above" (page 59), "St. Vincent's" (page 71), "For Julia, in the Deep Water" (page 74), "Aspects of Lilac" (page 75), "Notes from the Castle" (page 77), "Elegy for Agatha Christie" (page 99), "The Going Away of Young People" (page 103), "Her Dream" (page 107), and "Midsummer, England" (page 108) are © 1976 by The New Yorker Magazine, Inc.

"Dutch" by Daniel Mark Epstein, originally selected from the Summer 1976 issue of *The American Scholar*, is from the collection of poems, *The Follies*, by Daniel Mark Epstein, published by the Overlook Press, Lewis Hollow Road, Woodstock, New York, © 1977 by Daniel Mark Epstein.

CONTENTS

Maxine Kumin: (*First Award*)	The Retrieval System	1
	The Atlantic Monthly—May	
Galway Kinnell: (*Second Award*)		
	Saint Francis and the Sow	3
	The New Yorker—March 22	
Dan Masterson: (*Third Award*)	For a Child Going Blind	4
	The New Yorker—June 28	
Michael Allen:	Working Through Roots	6
	Minnesota Review—ns 7, Fall	
James Anderson:	Running It Down	7
	Poetry Northwest—Summer	
David Barton:	In the Heron's Sleep	8
	Poetry Northwest—Autumn	
Patricia Beer:	Parson Hawker's Farewell	9
	The Listener (England)—August	
Thomas Blackburn:	Dolomite	11
	The London Magazine (England)—December	
P. C. Bowman:	Grandfather in Springtime	13
	Lyric—Fall	
Alan Britt:	Prelude 1	14
	Northwest Review—Vol. XV, No. 3	
Edwin Brock:	Coming Home	15
	Ambit (England)—66	
Jack Butler:	Not Quite Like Son	17
	Poetry Northwest—Spring	
Michael Cameron:	Portrait of a Wolverine	18
	The Fiddlehead (Canada)—Summer	
Hayden Carruth:	Late Sonnet	20
	Poetry Northwest—Winter 75/76	
David Citino:	The Thing	21
	The Beloit Poetry Journal—Winter 75/76	
Cal Clothier:	November the Second	23
	Anglo-Welsh Review (Wales)—Autumn	
Denise Coelho:	Street Accident	25
	Assegai Two (England)	

Michael Collier:	Bathing	26
	The New Orleans Review—Vol. 5, No. 2	
M. R. Doty:	Lorenzo	27
	The New Orleans Review—Vol. 5, No. 1	
Philip Dow:	Song	29
	The New Yorker—May 3	
Peter Kane Dufault:	Burden	30
	The New Yorker—September 2	
Loren Eiseley:	Knossus	31
	Poetry—September	
Daniel Mark Epstein:	Dutch	33
	The American Scholar—Summer	
James Fenton:	In a Notebook	35
	New Statesman (England)—January	
S. L. Friedman:	The Displaced	37
	Epos—Vol. 26, No. 3	
Carol Frost:	A Woman with Her Plants Talking	38
	Prairie Schooner—Spring	
Stephen Gardner:	Adam's Dream	39
	Poetry Northwest—Summer	
Don Gordon:	Excavations	40
	Harper's—January	
Linda Gregerson:	Norway	41
	Field—Spring	
Kurt Heinzelman:	Fear a Joke Inside	43
	Poetry—May	
John Herman:	I Live In Terror of Arriving There	45
	Epos—Vol. 26, No. 3	
Daryl Hine:	The Aftermath	46
	The Georgia Review—Fall	
Daryl Hine:	Blight on Elm	48
	The New Yorker—September 13	
Charles Hobday:	The Dancers	50
	Orbis (England)—Spring	
Ted Hughes:	As I Came, I Saw a Wood	51
	Critical Quarterly (England)—Spring	
Ted Hughes:	Two Horses	52
	The London Magazine (England)—June	

Kate Jennings:	Place Names	55
	The American Scholar—Vol. 45, No. 3—Summer	
Marilyn Johnson:	Joseph	57
	Field—Fall	
Maxine Kumin:	Henry Manley, Living Alone, Keeps Time	58
	The New Yorker—October 4	
Maxine Kumin:	Splitting Wood at Six Above	59
	The New Yorker—January 2	
Greg Kuzma:	The Home Place	61
	The American Scholar—Vol. 45, No. 4—Autumn	
Greg Kuzma:	Sentences	62
	Prairie Schooner—Vol. 49, No. 4—Winter	
Dorothy Livesay:	Every Woman You Loved	65
	Queen's Quarterly (Canada)—Spring	
Edward Lowbury:	Vision	66
	New Statesman (England)—August	
Charles Martin:	Sharks at the New York Aquarium	67
	Poetry—January	
Molly McKaughan:		
	Fairy Tale of an Old Fashioned Daughter	68
	Northwest Review—Vol. XV, No. 3	
Hugh McKinley:	"... In Many Bodies."	70
	Bitterroot—Vol. XV, No. 55—Spring	
W. S. Merwin:	St. Vincent's	71
	The New Yorker—December 13	
John N. Morris:	For Julia, in the Deep Water	74
	The New Yorker—October 25	
Howard Moss:	Aspects of Lilac	75
	The New Yorker—May 10	
Howard Moss:	Notes from the Castle	77
	The New Yorker—August 30	
Mary Oliver:	New England Landscape	79
	Yankee—September	
Mary Oliver:	Poem for My Father's Ghost	81
	Prairie Schooner—Vol. 50, No. 3	
Paul Petrie:	The Explorers	83
	Poetry—October	

Jarold Ramsey:	Immersion	84
	The Atlantic Monthly—May	
Priscilla Stewart Randolph:	My Twelve Godchildren	85
	Epos—Vol. 26, No. 3	
Ira Sadoff:	The Ancestors and What They Left	88
	Northwest Review—Vol. XV, No. 3	
Margaret Scott:	Visiting the Maternity Hospital	90
	Quadrant (Australia)—October	
Graham Seal:	Man into Billiard Ball	91
	Outposts (England)—Summer	
Robert B. Shaw:	A Man and His Watch	92
	Poetry—July	
Robert Siegel:	To Market, to Market	94
	Prairie Schooner—Spring	
Dave Smith:	Back River Winter	96
	The Hudson Review—Spring	
Radcliffe Squires:	Some Marvelous Quarry	98
	The Hudson Review—Summer	
Pamela Stewart:	Elegy for Agatha Christie	99
	The New Yorker—May 3	
John Stone:	A Cliché Poem for Your Leaving	101
	The American Scholar—Summer	
Mary Swander:	Sweater	102
	The Ohio Review—Winter	
Eleanor Ross Taylor:	The Going Away of Young People	103
	The New Yorker—September 2	
Charles Tomlinson:	Macduff	105
	The Times Literary Supplement (England)—January	
Nance Van Winckel:	Salmon Fishing	106
	The Fiddlehead (Canada)—Spring	
David Wagoner:	Her Dream	107
	The New Yorker—January 6	
Derek Walcott:	Midsummer, England	108
	The New Yorker—February 9	
Ronald Wallace:	Installing the Bees	110
	Poetry—March	
Andrew Waterman:	From the Other Country	111
	The London Magazine (England)—Aug./Sept.	

Tom Wayman:	Grandmother	113
	The American Review, 24—April	
Miller Williams:		
	Why God Permits Evil for Answer To This Question of Interest to Many Write Bible Answers Dept. E–7	115
	The Southern Review—Summer	
Eleanor Wilner:	A Private Space	117
	The Minnesota Review—Spring	
Eleanor Wilner:	Knowing the Enemy	119
	The Minnesota Review—Spring	

THE RETRIEVAL SYSTEM

It begins with my dog, now dead, who all his long life
carried about in his head the brown eyes of my father,
keen, loving, accepting, sorrowful, whatever;
they were Daddy's all right, handed on, except
for their phosphorescent gleam tunneling the night
which I have to concede was a separate gift.

Uncannily when I'm alone these features
come up to link my lost people
with the patient domestic beasts of my life. For example,
the wethered goat who runs free in pasture and stable
with his flecked, agate eyes and his minus-sign pupils
blats in the tiny voice of my former piano teacher

whose bones beat time in my dreams and whose terrible breath
soured *Country Gardens, Humoresque,* and unplayable Bach.
My elderly aunts, wearing the heads of willful
intelligent ponies, stand at the fence begging apples.
The sister who died at three has my cat's faint chin,
my cat's inscrutable squint, and cried catlike in pain.

I remember the funeral. *The Lord is my shepherd,*
we said. I don't want to brood. Fact: it is people who fade,
it is animals that retrieve them. A boy
I loved once keeps coming back as my yearling colt,
cocksure at the gallop, racing his shadow
for the hell of it. He runs merely to be.
A boy who was lost in the war thirty years ago
and buried at sea.

Here, it's forty degrees and raining. The weatherman
who looks like my resident owl, the one who goes out and in
by the open haymow, appears on the TV screen.
With his heart-shaped face, he is also my late dentist's double,
donnish, bifocaled, kind. Going a little gray,
advising this wisdom tooth will have to come out someday,

meanwhile filling it as a favor. Another save.
It outlasted him. The forecast is nothing but trouble.
It will snow fiercely enough to fill all these open graves.

MAXINE KUMIN

SAINT FRANCIS AND THE SOW

The bud
stands for all things,
even for those things that don't flower,
because everything flowers from within, of self-blessing.
Though sometimes it's necessary
to reteach a thing its loveliness,
to put a hand on its brow
of the flower
and retell it in words and in touch
it is lovely
until it flowers again from within, of self-blessing.
As Saint Francis
put his hand on the creased forehead
of the sow, and told her in words and in touch
blessings of earth on the sow, and the sow
began remembering all down her thick length,
from the earthen snout all the way through the fodder and slops
to the spiritual curl of the tail,
from the hard spininess spiked out from the spine
down through the great, unbreakable heart
to the sheer blue milken dreaminess shuddering and squirting
from the fourteen teats into the fourteen mouths sucking and
    blowing beneath them:
the long, perfect loveliness of sow.

GALWAY KINNELL

FOR A CHILD GOING BLIND

I have awakened her
when the sky was at its blackest,
all stars erased, no moon to speak of,
and led her down the front path
to our dock, where we'd swim to the raft,
finding it by touch
fifty or sixty strokes from shore.

And sit
listening to things, the movement of water
around us drawing us closer, a hunched
double knot of child and father
hearing all there is to hear,
close beneath bats who see without sight,
whose hunger is fed by darkness.

The neighbors see her often in the woods,
on hands and knees, smoothing the moss
where it spreads in the shade, marvelling
at the tongues of birds, the stained petal
of the dogwood, the vein of color
skirting the edge of an upturned stone.

This morning she awoke to the first flash
of the magnolia, and will save the petals
as they fall, their purpled lids
curling white on the lawn.

We meant to tell her how the rainbows come,
how they close into shadows,
how we would be there nonetheless;
we meant to tell her before
they arrived at supper this evening,
rimming everything in sight.

She wonders if we see them
cupping the stars, the kitchen lamp,
each other's face, and we say
we do.

    DAN MASTERSON

WORKING THROUGH ROOTS

for Sonya and Jim

I work the east field in the afternoon.
There is sun in the cool haze in the west.
As I shovel the soft, sandy field, I can hear
cedar and wild rose, scrub oak,
and the pain in the small root pores.
There's a flutter of rabbit and birds to my right.
I am their dream in the hot day.
I am facing north on this soft hill.
The soil is grey feather and warns me that walking
in this place can uncover places
that have seldom been twined in sleep.

I work the vineyard and am proud of the sweat
in the red bandana on my forehead.

I work against roots: flat-tongued prickly weed,
pokeweed, poison ivy. I shovel them up,
cut off the roots and feel the opening sand.
I am making room for Cabernet Sauvignon.
There will soon be a thousand green heads
that will round themselves into the deepest purple.

The roots are like worms,
a form of love between sky and ground.
Just as a river is the long way for a mountain
to feed the sea.

MICHAEL ALLEN

RUNNING IT DOWN

Running it down. The serpentine once-over then
Sighting the damn thing in. All so extremely
easy you wonder why you have waited so long.
There. Just a little to the left
near the crease that marks the center
of the hood.
The look of recognition will last only a moment.
The glance up as you stare down
And then:
You run the damn thing down.
Down as you have done a hundred times in dreams
later waking fit for the day
turning sour before the first break, and
down as you have done countless times as
conversations drifted
And you imagined just the slightest thump.
Now you will do it. Then drive on
as if nothing happened and no one saw.
Running it down. The easiest thing in the world.
The look of recognition will only last a moment.
The rest of your life will be lived content.
The days you have will spend like stolen money.
The men and women you know will sense something great.
The cry in the dream will come from the next apartment.
Others will be the ones who bend beneath themselves.

JAMES ANDERSON

IN THE HERON'S SLEEP

In the heron's sleep
and the white crow's stare,
near houses built
on the breakneck strand,
in tidal froth and garden ditch,
in earthly fires
and the terrors of the air,
in heavens holier
than the sea-cresting moon
that undermines the sky,

straw stalks and towers fall,
the cove life crumbles
and the furry-eared owls
turn their eyes
on Wellfleet's trembling tide,
while in the back yards
rabbit clans hew and whisk,
fog burns off,
old bees throng the goldenrod
and these white buds glow

like risen souls, fierce,
sharp as harvest tines,
their tips
an intricate sea-sucked hue,
their stem-feathers slanting
higher than the stem,
their roots washed clean
as any earthly daughter could be,
their smallest cells turning bright
and blonde with praise.

DAVID BARTON

PARSON HAWKER'S FAREWELL

Let no one wear black at my funeral.
I have not let blackness be the friend
To me it could have been. The black storm
Crawling with demons clambered up the sky
Each day. My eyes shrank. I turned away
And the prince demon tore the roof off my house.

I have passed through purple and grey to white.
I am as white now as the ship's figurehead
The sea spat out on the shore one day.
All its paint licked off, it had a body
Still, better without gaudiness, a face
Hinting at what was behind the colours.

I have been compassionate at the lych-gate.
I have been made hateful by drowned sailors
Brought to me every one, some in good clothes
Others piecemeal out of the murk of rock pools
Where the biting and shaking sea at last left them,
Limbs, dispossessed hearts, all begging for burial.

Those storms. 'A corpse ashore, sir.' The words
Make me cringe even as the gap narrows
Between me and the men I every day sent
To resurrection. All ended with me, and I
Have been alone. Even my loving wife cannot
Ward off the blown leaves that presage storm.

My fellow clerics care mostly about food.
They eat pigs' faces: cannibals, narcissists.
With gluttony they disgust their own angels.
What can I call them? Some Latin name
With a prim mouth and filth in the tail.
They know enough for that. Pigs' faeces might do.

You see, I have rage still. At lifeboatmen
At coroners I have raged, at those who stole
My books, at the demons who chewed up my fields
Forcing me to buy corn. I shall always
Be angry but perhaps with a white heat
That seraphim will sociably glare back at.

Farewell to the bad roads and the steep hills
And London remote. I shall never walk
On the cliffs alone again. My last cats
Whose language I spoke fluently will outlive me.
Peace and defiance be with you all. What matters
Is not money or being feasted but soul safe.

PATRICIA BEER

DOLOMITE

Some five steep miles from the old town of Belluno,
At the Casa Bortot we drank wine and looked at the river, Piave,
Humming in silence on the afternoon of Italian summer,
Then heaved on our packs and started for the rifugio.
The climbers' track ran high over a stream from the mountain,
Its stones polished by winter's great water
Fuming down from the glacier of the Schiara,
As we sweated in the scent of pines and the gentian.

Then, after two hours, the track ran down to
A flatness of the stream-bed where we drank and rested
And I smeared your feet with soap as you said they ached,
Then the last precipitous, grinding hour to the rifugio.
It was dusk when we reached it and heard the sound of voices
Of three or four Austrians smoking on the balcony—
"*Grüss Gott*"—then we met the custodian and his wife and their baby,
At seeing old friends one rejoices.

That night we were woken up by the glare of lightning
And got out of our bunks to watch it illuminate
Each detail of the orange, enormous Dolomite
But there was no thunder to suggest storm and giants fighting
And at five o'clock we ate bread and drank black coffee.
It must be twenty years now but the details are insoluble,
And death will not blur the customary that is memorable,
And you were then, as this night, most beautiful to me.

On the way to the climb and its start by the Portala,
Black lizards crawled too repulsive to be eaten by living creature
And I recall picking out the particular feature
For which we were using the Via Ferrata, Il Gusella della Schiara,
The meaning of being then and our destiny
The "crux" of the mountain and some two hundred feet high.
Far below we heard the bells of grazing sheep.

On the top of the needle that was by no means easy,
Guides had rivetted a cross of iron,
Memento of our situation and destination.
We reached the slabs again by a third abseil,
And walked down to the hut after reclimbing the Via Ferrata,
In the high, solar glare of the later noon.
Never again will I step so lightly under this sun;
Before we ate and drank wine we took stinging grappa.

Strange how some moments that were "now" can never finish.
Here I blend a climb out of many climbs that illuminated
The monotony of events long gone and quite faded,
But these like love, communion, art, do not perish.
And so on my sixtieth birthday I celebrate the instant,
That has no end to its ceremony of delight—
We mean we are nearer the dawn when we say "It's late;"
Where is there an end to it, the imperdurable moment?

         THOMAS BLACKBURN

GRANDFATHER IN SPRINGTIME

His hands rest together like the involute crocus,
Saffron-colored and waiting for a bit of heat
On a bed of McIntosh plaid;
A child now, he is wholly glad,
Here in the garden where death and life compete
Over each gardenia bush, to watch the hocus-pocus
Of light striking random color from the earth

And to think on those Amazons of the field who give birth
And in the same motion cut a swath of grain;
With the long, cruel wind and unwind
Of serpentine scythes swept around
The newborns are rocked to their rest, and the fine
Yellow-haired stalks shift once with their pain:
Each sheaf sighs *ahimsa!* as it hits the ground.

P. C. Bowman

PRELUDE 1

It is not the battle, my stupid friend,
but the wounds that bother us.
Stars break off at their stalks
and churn our blood cells into fine dust.
It is not the word, which we never understood anyway,
but the voice muffled by shirt collars.
The voice with its little hooves
leaps from the body pinned to a chair.
Of how the hands collapse with rage,
tiny camp fires ignite along the face.
Our legs begin to hum inside this room
the blood at last sprouts wings.
I have waited for this moment often enough
for the entire body to shake itself from sleep.
But as usual in matters such as this
we are too slow and a bird dies in our lungs.
We are satisfied with the couplet or the razor,
an electric light sways in a farmhouse kitchen.
But of course, it is not our friendships
that are at stake here, they have been bulldozed
through the corridors as it is; no it is something
more precious than even that, something so close
to ourselves that it hardly exists at all,
it is a very old man chipping flint near a damp field,
at times he pauses and looks over his shoulder,
or it might not be that at all,
perhaps it is only a young girl
raking dead leaves across our blood.

ALAN BRITT

COMING HOME

Woman, you were magnificent in the rocks
and wild water, so that almost I forgot
you were away and shouted you out
in the spray and the grey-white limestone.
But it was lonely in the bay: our train
swam the sea whipped up by wind
and spotted by storm-drops and you spat
white horses like insults at me.

Woman, in Lancaster you left me among
the muck-coloured fields sucking rain
not thirstily but like a boozer with
a tenth pint. Until, entering Wigan,
you came back with flat vowels
under black streaming roofs,
made a home from a one-roomed hovel and
stared out the pinch-cheeked curly creatures.

Spreading yourself into the Midlands
you were the way Matisse laid pink
on green: almost you were gone
or, rather, you were so diffused
that I could find no opening to you
but slept and waited. In light-hearted Ely
you sang the cathedral effortlessly
and among Thetford's conifers
sharpened your notes for Christmas.

Now, thank God, we are together with
your familiar warm flesh glowing;
similes and metaphors stay strung out
along the wet tracks from us to Cumbria.
Woman, that language is gone: it is
the words I use in separation
not speaking myself nor, really, you
but a charm which hurts, a hairshirt,
needles in a wax brain looking
for the distraction of acupuncture.

My love, it is no longer dialogue but
myself entering you again and again
to make this beginning which is this
becoming which is this continuous end.

EDWIN BROCK

NOT QUITE LIKE SON

Einstein's son is dead, who studied sediment,
God bless his courage. He knew more
About the way the water met the shore
Or buckled off some derelict impediment
Than anyone had known before.

His father's differential gaze almost, almost
Undid the final lucid veil:
So we'll recall it till the yarn goes stale.
Would it have been the blazing focus of that Ghost,
Too terrible to fade or fail?

Or pools of zero, like the little virtual o's
Swirls breed in puddles at noonday,
That swarm, and freckle, and seem almost to play,
False pupils on wrinkled sand? How should we suppose,
Who hardly know enough to say

How two skeins of meat can connect us to the sun?
—Light crawls down sewers to the brain
But keeps a cleanliness that none explain.
He proved nothing, but brought, watery, trembling, one
Frail field to almost total gain.

God bless his son, who shaped no legend for himself,
But made himself useful, and gave
Plain counsel on the sunken limestone cave,
The running wave rumpled on the continental shelf,
And the wave standing off the wave.

JACK BUTLER

PORTRAIT OF A WOLVERINE

It comes out of this snapshot
snout first, the twitching curl of liver
nosing through last year's smells,
almost alive, a mangy terrorist
breaking through the green spines of balsam.
A face follows, blackened as if charred
in the coals of some carnage,
with all of it, the muzzle, the poked little
eyes, the disagreement, forced around
a horrible grin hanging
down like a rapist's after-yawn.
Look closer: the phrase of incisors,
yellowish through red, is
a clue: the discolouration between them
wasn't living when the jaws met in it,
it was turned down by everything
hunting the muskeg except this,
this degenerate bear patched together
from the nightmares of Eskimos.
And is it living after all?
: moving down the skull
to the faded forehead and the nude
pink bat's ears, the whole head
(hung as if ashamed or choking)
harsh as a voodoo mask
carved in anthracite, and as cold.
It looks to be too much
for the scrawny neck, just as the shoulders
shouldn't still connect with the neck
yawing away to the left and right of the scent
enough to snap a goose-neck lamp.
The trunk has no shape; shit-coloured,
ragged as something in a diseased fur coat,
it is the opposite of rodents
being darker, blacker on the paunch and legs
than on the back, as if refusing camouflage

or existing outside evolution.
And maybe it is. Cannibal, striped like a convict,
undisguised, with no enemies,
that hauls its perverse steel whisk of a tail
to sweep up everything behind
except the cadaverous reek of its anus.
Maybe it doesn't need to be quiet, finally,
lonely as something dead,
snuffling obscenely over the ice-fields
on 4 bloated paws fanged with crampons of bone.
It comes out of this snapshot
like a ghoul's memory, past redemption,
more terrible for being small,
crossing the vast archipelagoes of darkness
that threaten the room you watch from.

MICHAEL CAMERON

LATE SONNET

For that the sonnet no doubt was my own true
singing and suchlike other song; for that
I gave it up half-coldheartedly to set
my lines in a fashion that proclaimed its virtue
original in young arrogant artificers who
had not my geniality nor voice and yet
their fashionableness was persuasive to me: what
shame and sorrow I pay!
                        And that I knew
that beautiful hot old man Sidney Bechet
and heard his music often but not what he
was saying, that tone, phrasing, and free play
of feeling mean more than originality,
these being the actual qualities of song.
Nor is it essential to be young.

                                                Hayden Carruth

THE THING

rubbing her neck and legs
he raised sparks of rapid breath
and beads of moisture deep within her.
everything in the car was soft with dew,
their mouths falling into each other.
they lost their minds in adolescent desperation.
it was natural then that, the radio being off,
they would not have heard
of the thing's glowing arrival,
its landing in a nearby forest,
of reports of unspeakable horrors,
its thirst for bread and flesh.
when the car began to rock
he thought it was her sixteen-year-old
happiness moving below him: the odor
he gave to her as well, feeling
he had tapped a deeper well
of musk and dark oil.
she thought, upon seeing it
all at once framed in the passenger window,
that it looked desperately like his mother;
he, that it bore a ferocity
akin only to her father.
their final seconds together
were spent in wild fright and passion,
locked together, lipless,
the horror breathing their own passions
upon the wet windows, part of something
no one could stop.

it would be left to someone else
to call out the army,
the wise men in white coats
who would try to kill this thing
with electricity or bacteria or fire
or kindness; they lay together
in the dark belly of a piece
of night sky, stilled for all time,
out of the picture, safe again.

DAVID CITINO

NOVEMBER THE SECOND

1

Death has appealed to you
for many years; for many years
every letter, every phone call has
centred on your wish that you were dead.

2

Now in death's purdah
veiled by the private stillness of your face
you lie and wait. You were always
far too impatient, far too early
to catch the train—all those hours
we wasted together on wintry platforms!

3

November the second.
It's Saturday morning for us (you have only
light and dark) and Mollie and I
sit keeping you company. As she knits
her needles tick-tock
with a steady but muted pulse.

4

I cannot speak for your eyes.
You hear what I say,
what I say to myself on your behalf;
but I cannot express what my eyes feel.
Your silence infects me, and you must not see
when my eyes cry out that you cannot speak.

5

Everything we do today
must seal itself to your memory,
must become symbolic, ceremonial.
Hot orbs of wax, the giant rose hips
glow against the dank autumn soil.

6

My memory hoards you, yearns
to remember you not as you now are
but as you will be
in your photographs.

7

The crescent of daylight
under your wedding ring waxes daily;
your finger thins in my hand
though your grip screams aloud
Hold me! Speak to me!—Eyes and hands
are all we can share
for my tongue is tied down to words.
Soon, soon the sightless fingers
are only a glove.

CAL CLOTHIER

STREET ACCIDENT

We are all he has at this moment.

The streetlight
spins filaments of rain about us,
holds us together
in a tight knot of concern.

Who he is does not matter.
We have already forgiven his recklessness.
Only his stillness
is important.

My finger dialled for him
his small hope of recovery.
Now he is ours
and those he loves
have yet a little time to be untroubled.

Soon the pulsating light
will come
bear him away on a blue shriek
deliver him
to the System and its tight-lipped ethics.

Who we were will not matter.

He will become again
nothing to us
who have no name to call him by.

       Denise Coelho

BATHING

The light in the bright yellow curtains
turns the counter novelties garish: my
husband's shaver, flat, electricless,
a dead reel for casting.

I spawn myself back in the warm languid
bath, alone, in an afternoon of backwash,
safe from the house that holds me like my
husband, tenderly and reasonable but dry.
Here, I close my eyes and feel a colorless
sheet rise to my chin and the water's turbulent
entrance at my feet.

Wet, I dream of fishes made from shells, carved
into the shape of scales and hinged together.
I see them in curio shops and on the
beach where Mexicans tempt me with them,
limp in their hands. They are as real as any
dead fish—a crafted death of well polished scales.

When the water drains (a ruffled sheet sucked off
my legs) I'm beached on the porcelain, and hear
the drain plug pop again and again
like a lead weight plunking hook and line—
it signals the end. I breathe rapidly.
The cool air barbs my skin.

I dehydrate completely in a towel
then let it fall like wet newspaper to
my feet. On a scale, behind the door,
I check my weight and view, full length,
my profile: the image I bleed for. In the
yellow light, my life as real as any death.

MICHAEL COLLIER

LORENZO

In the beginning I was indifferent to you
you offered me an orange
I ordered more purple ink
you sat at your desk
I in my rocker
in the same room
we watched dark Iowa's mad heart grow cold

Then I began to hate you
I don't know why
I wrote of it to my brother
& when it was over
you would come in saying one morning
something banal on a sunny day
& I wanted to protect you

So I pretended not to see you
in your red sandals & straw hat
blazing in the art center
with your apostle's spoon
& the trembling cub in your arms

I am growing old
though I am younger than you
when you ride by
in your Princess Anne t-shirt
& your new blue collars
I think what a bonny rider
& what a fine set of glad bells

Now I think I've come to love you
you are brittle & fairylike
long as darkly sung timber
seabark and aspidellian
a white oar some lark lives in

I tell your wife you are shooting pool
she too is growing old
but we listen all of us
to the ankles of that young girl crack
as she comes to you through the snow like a wolf

Sleeping beside my husband
he'll say Ah what wisteria they'll be
gathering in the old places
& what foxfires they'll be finding
in the hollow trees
but I'll say have you ever heard
such bells in the Midwestern night
& such voices thrashing in the rain

Protect him then he'll say
but remember first of all he's an Irishman

Being the Indian you are
in the fall when the first snow returns
you'll hand me an orange
& I'll take the overwhelming
dried up thing and say

Take your bride out tonight Lorenzo
I'll sit with your wife
we'll watch the hawks lean
over the fields
rise to the apron of the moon

& she'll take out her silver scissors
and the hawks will be riding on the stars

Their bloody wings broken against the corn

And she will say Lorenzo Lorenzo
I wanted so not to stop you

M. R. Doty

SONG

What binds the atom together
must be like these hives,
this cluster of white bee boxes near the creek,
this exhaling and breathing of wings
like sparks, bits of a mirror,
tracing over the meadow
the petals of a transparent blossom
                          opening—

these veins flow into a dark armature,
heart or brain, a globular,
interior mirror
of ignited cells about which
the mind whirls: this sibilant,
            luminous pulp,
                      one cell
or one cell's shadow
        in the great body of growing
                      we grow in.

PHILIP DOW

BURDEN

I called you because I could not stand alone
looking north to that skyline-
tree globed with its yellow apples
balancing like a fountain of planets
in the bright light and the blue air.

And because on the way there
I looked at a smooth cirque
the brook had worn in a stone;
and nothing as soft as water
could, by taking care,
have so pestled and polished
that granite mortar, only
by a thousand years of indifference,
of aiming elsewhere.

I wish we might do—or no,
look back and find we had done—
some unadvertised thing
overwhelming and un-self-aware
as water streamlining a stone, or a tree's
kindling in an empty meadow
its casual Hesperides.

     PETER KANE DUFAULT

KNOSSUS

"The Kefti come no more.
They bear us no more the oils
and the cedars for coffins.
Their sails are lost." This was their epitaph
along with the recorded black sky and the ashfall.
Then Egypt forgot the gracious isle of the olives
and the palaces of the seven kings
where athletes somersaulted
over the spread horns of bulls.

They died in one night, the pillars of the palace buckling,
great stones cast down, the galleys
beached on the shore, ruin and ashes
assailing men from the sky.
Thera, the burst throat of the world, coughing fire and
    brimstone
there to the north, its voice like the bellowing of a
    loosed god
long propitiated to no purpose.
We have known it in our own lives—
the fear of the moving atoms, but these people
endured the actual megaton explosion, and their
    remnants
faded from history, while the timeless, practical
    Egyptians
regretted a small loss of trade.

Civilizations die as men die, by accident then.
I have seen on an old maple stump
a sapling attempt to grow.
The Kefti come no more,
but here the excavated amphorae
stand by the palace walls waiting
and the beautiful art
is known in the books of the world.
Something lingers in the air as though it would speak.
The waters are bright blue.

I, whose people were horned barbarians,
admire what was done here. I do not think,
in the rain of the fire to come, we will leave anything
   so precious.
Who will bother to scratch after us upon stone the
   regretful words,
"They come no more."

Loren Eiseley

DUTCH

Dutch in the wire cage, burning away with electrified stylus
    or working the dye in slow along the pinpricks
a handful of flesh at a time. High musk
of burnt flesh like the back street meat markets.
       He is some kind of artist.

My mother thought otherwise, jerking coke at the bar;
    six months out of the flatlands
she married into this garden of earthly delights:
    the ninth street shooting gallery, peep show carnival
and Dutch the tattooist,
a living advertisement of his own genius
              and the skill of his masters,
not a square foot of unadorned flesh on his whole body.

She would lead the drunk boys out by the elbow,
    whispering "this is no way to prove yourself a man,"
recalling her uncle Mack raving drunk
    clawing at vein-blue snakes drawn up his arms,
or a tale her sailor father told
        of a Swedish boy shy of the needle,
who dreamed his fear out loud
    and woke tangled in the ship's hammock,
twisted in a nightmare and the crew knew it.
And how they pitched in to get the young Swede drunk
    and strapped him to the mess table
and hired a French tattooist
aboard with his packet of needles and rare dyes.
He worked a great clipper ship on the boy's chest
    with full rigging
where wind would catch full in the sails when the blood cleared.

My mother would lead them away from the wire cage

while her father-in-law shouted to his son from the cash register:
    "You bring a *shiksa* into a place of business..."
and mother:
        "What kind of a Jew grows rich
            from writing on a man's body?
      Your laws cry out against it."
And the old man again:
"We are not Gods to make our laws for other men."

I write on your clean skin, my people
    and then dream the world will see you as you were made.

                                Daniel Mark Epstein

IN A NOTEBOOK

There was a river overhung with trees
With wooden houses built along its shallows
From which the morning sun drew up a haze
And the gyrations of the early swallows
Paid no attention to the gentle breeze
Which spoke discreetly from the weeping willows.
There was a jetty by the forest clearing
Where a small boat was tugging at its mooring.

And night still lingered underneath the eaves.
In the dark houseboats families were stirring
And Chinese soup was cooked on charcoal stoves.
Then one by one there came into the clearing
Mothers and daughters bowed beneath their sheaves.
The silent children gathered round me staring
And the shy soldiers setting out for battle
Asked for a cigarette and laughed a little.

From low canoes old men laid out their nets
While on the bank young boys with lines were fishing.
The wicker traps were drawn up by their floats.
The girls stood waist-deep in the river washing
Or tossed the day's rice on enamel plates
And I sat drinking bitter coffee wishing
The tide would turn, to bring me to my senses
After the pleasant war and the evasive answers.

There was a river overhung with trees.
The girls stood waist-deep in the river washing,
And night still lingered underneath the eaves
While on the bank young boys with lines were fishing.
Mothers and daughters bowed beneath their sheaves
While I sat drinking bitter coffee wishing—
And the tide turned and brought me to my senses.
The pleasant war brought the unpleasant answers:

The villages are burnt, the cities void;
The morning light has left the river view;
The distant followers have been dismayed;
And I'm afraid, reading this passage now
That everything I knew has been destroyed
By those whom I admired but never knew;
The laughing soldiers fought to their defeat
And I'm afraid most of my friends are dead.

JAMES FENTON

THE DISPLACED

The children brush against the window pane:
they are light as wax
their fingers taper into mist
they drop like tears
they cannot find their fathers
I see their bones through the sheer skin

There are too many of them
they exhaust our love
they have no claim

I have mailed a dutiful donation
I must escape the transparent skin
the dark cavernous eyes
I am not responsible for the state of the world
I am not responsible
I ask to be relieved

I saw only a mist of children
nebulous as light
slip past the pane

S. L. Friedman

A WOMAN WITH HER PLANTS TALKING

People keep giving me plants.
I must be loved, surreal. Succulents.
I stole the asparagus fern from my tenant,
potted it for my green bedroom.
The mother plant molded and coated the bulbs
like tongues in the dirt. The tenant has handsome legs.
I water the little green animals
who push up their bare heads gratefully
then talk in long vowels in the wet air.

The men with white veins for feet.
Plants with beards or double chins.
Today for a lamp, I have more friends.
The humid soil, their dirt up my fingernails,
the lovely card table by the window that eats sun
for them and smiles. The striped tiger upstairs.
What polished ivy creeps
on my arm—a badgered pet?
The male tiger in the rafters.
The fern sticks on my pillow, moss pillow,
and winds its vegetable feet nearer
knowing it is not a caterpillar.
If the bed would just make itself fold
to swallow me. To die in secretions.
I buck in that satin shell,
try to break the jungle. Come orange tiger.
By day I shine all their leaves,
see my face hundreds of times as if in dark pictures.

CAROL FROST

ADAM'S DREAM

In the last male hour
Warm with the change of his sleep
She came from outside his mind

In a birth he could not have known.
Around him were shapes he had named:
Solid tree, quick deer, trusting sheep.

Yet this was something more,
Sliding down the curve of his back,
A hand that wasn't his on his side.

Before this soft light turned the earth
He had lain in his dreams without fear.
But the terror that rests in us now

Sprang then for the first time in him.
The forest floor rolled with a heat
He sensed, but without name or form,

And the sun framed the world new again.
And the garden he lived in had died.

STEPHEN GARDNER

EXCAVATIONS

I am haunted by the futile sound
Of digging in the buried cities
Of the world,
By the intent face of the science
Of bones, stones, and feathers.

Vainly the heart of a people
Is sought in the kitchen midden.
It vanishes whether the end comes
As smallpox, or lava flow, or drought,
Or the barbarian riding his stallion
Up the mosaic stairs.

Discover in what artifacts
The boy's love or fear of his father,
The girl diminished by the mother,
The man and the woman in the solitude
Of the stars of the historic night;

Or the exercise of the power
Or the paramount chief,
Or the relation between the entrails
And the beginning of wars
And the drowning of virgins.

It existed for a fragment of time
In an ambience of its own desire.
Who digs in the curious plateau
Releases it forever like myrrh
Escaping with a sigh
The gold coffin of the king.

Don Gordon

NORWAY

Fishbone ground for cleaning, flagstone
halls, girls who wear gray dresses
scrub them blind. It takes a lot of friction,
smoothing stones, your knees grow scales.
When I come back the girls are gone,
my bed is straight and smells of fish.

> This is where she used to work and this
> is where she's buried.

Stone and water stint a farm, grudge
foothold. One white horse,
reluctant pasture. Go high enough
the rocks aren't even good for hiding.
Tunnels can't be dug and so they're
built, some wooden slats to help
with all that snow and sky.

> And this is what she looked like,
> this is how we knew you right away.

Whalemeat has more blood
than anything that grows on land.
Three days without rain in Bergen
this year, hands hung, mouths hung.
The people get in boats one night
each June and watch the sun
dip down, dip up again. That's festival,
the rest is oilcloth, heavy nets.
In boots like these you only step
on purpose; winters, no one talks.

> And this is where you'll sleep, we
> haven't used the pillows since she left.

Cloudberries kjenner du? the children
pick them, bowls filled up and spilling over.
I've a chair to learn a language in,
the chair's too soft, my memory's wrong,
I rock instead. Outside the grammar's strict,
the square is all right angles, steps,
a fountain blows the pavement wet.
A tall man crosses on his way to class,
he has no family, walks
a line as dazzling as Pythagoras.

        And this, you may not want to wear it,
        is for you to keep.

                LINDA GREGERSON

FEAR A JOKE INSIDE

It is said that Benjamin Franklin did not author the Declaration of Independence because the Founding Fathers were afraid he might conceal a joke somewhere inside it.

1

*In the indirection of human events
It sometimes becomes necessary for
The first man to manage a bold hand
Even a mad king could not misunderstand.*

2

Warming his feet by the stove,
The possible republic takes
    The shape of his mind. He fashions
The invented country into flakes

Of fire taking shape about
His feet. His declaration will
    Constitute a chronicle,
Not of heaven on a hill,

But of a possibly good man
In a reasonable land,
    Like this room, this fire, this
Armed rocker which is wholly his.

3

Well-heeled but with an honest streak, a proper
Printer and a prince's welcome guest,
Lover of women, fondly tied to none,
Who reasons with the best and counts his change,
He remembers the rain, and pokes the fire.
Learning at last to be humble, he writes about the sun
Setting and rising on the President's chair.
The spectacled eye recalls the storm,
What natural threatenings of the air
One does and does not expect to be
Struck by, earning in the end through the lightning
The peace of holding on, listening for fear
Inside. In his own small hand he invents
The state of his mind, a self-evident
Commonwealth innocent of weather.
Laurel stars the slopes of his capitol;
About the veined walls of his chambers
The history of the nation is printed in smoke
As his finger moves through the ashes
Like the shriven tongue of an Indian, and his ring
Makes a little light through the belled corridors
Like a key on a string, bearing the inscription of fire.

      KURT HEINZELMAN

I LIVE IN TERROR OF ARRIVING THERE

I live in terror of arriving there,
Crossing the frontier into alien air,
Without my passport, with my passport bare;

So that behind me, a dried honeycomb,
The labyrinthine region of our home
Stretches away, a barren decatome,

Where instantly the mountain and the rose
Are stilled together in a like repose,
And nothing comes and nothing ever goes,

But all lie frozen: tower, sea, and town
Lie lapsed together in a single frown
Of shifting shadow where the light pours down.

But Nothing beats about them, and its flame
Licks at the light and shadow with the same
Remorseless silence on that endless plain.

And coming to the keeper of that place
A dread will seize me that his common face
Reflects the visage of my own disgrace;

And that behind me where the common city
Burns on the human plain, the home of pity
Was left behind me irrevocably,

And now we bear the burden of our shame:
Our own accreted share of praise or blame
Is scrivened now as our eternal name.

O save me from this terror and this dread,
Nights of long labor for the living bread!
And claim me for the living from the dead.

JOHN HERMAN

THE AFTERMATH

1

Psychology was Psyche's fault:
The bedside lamp, the burning drop
She let fall upon the flawless
Shoulder of the unconscious god.
For a moment though she saw him
Almost as he was, soft not hard
As she had always known him in the dark,
His nakedness no longer unashamed
But vulnerable as a mortal
Lost in a dream, the midnight black
Of his hair about the secret face
Of love: only for a moment
Before the immortal god
Woke and knew her and flew away.

2

His departure an epiphany,
The work of night, without a word
Of apology he went away
As it was written, by another way
Into his own country. Boy or bird,
There for the time being he will stay.
In valediction what was she to say?
For all her insight Psyche cannot say
Candidly she understood his stay
Although offended by its brevity.
Was her anxiety absurd
In the light of yesterday?
Humiliated and bewildered,
She will follow anyway.

3
Above the unintelligible
Pack with human faces,
Wings like parentheses
Stuck upon his back,
He hovered out of reach,
Taunting and afraid,
Abruptly fallible,
Frantic to escape
The trap of consciousness.
What did his flight portend?
Faith might have divined.
Without an informing myth,
Bored beyond belief,
Psyche can only guess.

4
Compared to daily life her other tasks
Were child's play: sorting out the letters
Of the infatuated alphabet
To spell the name of her mistake;
Fetching refreshment from the dead;
The sort of tests that one is set in nightmare,
A bedtime story or an allegory,
Which must be solved before you wake,
Penitences possible except
Her final labor, to forget
The stolen sight of Love in bed
Beside her, naked and asleep,
The moving shadow on his cheek,
His surprised look before he fled.

DARYL HINE

BLIGHT ON ELM

Did they have to go, our shady neighbors,
Before we even got to know their names?
Lofty, supercilious, but kind,
You never saw their faces in the papers
Although they flirted with the wind
Frequently and flagrantly enough
And were no strangers to the sun or rain.

Embarrassed gods, silent branch factories,
Their loss leaves a lacuna in the landscape
Shocked and shattered by their disappearance.
Decimated by a radical disease,
Almost unnoticed there they stood
Year in, year out, along the streets
To which as well as shade they gave their names.

Individuals of a species
Whose autumn was an age of gold,
They grew unconscious in the forest
We infer from all these trees,
Survivors of the primal wood.
We used to think that form determined matter
But now we see that matter dictates form.

Remember how we used to watch them change
Their drip-dry garments spring and fall
From green to brown and back again?
This is how the suburbs lose their cool
By a coincidence never really strange,
The end in view is nearly natural,
The beautiful laid level with the plain.

Destroyers came to get them about dawn
Having well beforehand marked each victim
With an X, they cut them down
And fed them limb by leafy limb
To an insatiable machine
Whose sinister mosquito whine
Now near, now far, annoys us all year long.

Their absence aches like an extracted tooth
We will learn to live without in time,
Truncated, a redundant proof,
As if we needed one, of death.
Only in the medium of dream
Does there exist an afterlife
Where they return and we regain our youth.

DARYL HINE

THE DANCERS

A panicking panting rabbit started up
Under my feet, with death in the shape of a stoat,
Black, sleek, inevitable, hot on his heels.
Both cut across my path and disappeared
Into the bracken. What small tragedy
Ensued I didn't see, but I could guess.
Death's never far away in the country,
Whether he stuffs a rabbit into his pot,
A blackbird gutted for a cat's amusement
Or a hedgehog flattened into the tarmac.

I saw myself twenty years before
Among the other peapickers converging
Like the legions round doomed Jerusalem
On the last green clump in the bareplucked field
And another rabbit scuttling between our shoes
From the last refuge to which we'd driven him.
A gipsy dived for his heels, tackled him, caught him,
Wrung his neck and stowed him in his pocket.

A mile or two on, in a stubble field
I found two hares dancing, leaping, curvetting
Like two half-drunk victorious rugger-players,
Mad as in March, though it was August now.
Ignoring me, who might have carried
A gun for all they knew, they kept on dancing,
Yet as country-dwellers hares know death
More intimately than we. I watched, admiring
Their philosophy: dance, boy, while you can.

Charles Hobday

AS I CAME, I SAW A WOOD

Where trees stood in dirt, clutching at the sky
Like savages photographed in the middle of a ritual
Birds danced among them and animals took part
Insects too and around their feet flowers

And time was not present they never stopped
Or left anything old or reached any new thing
Everything moved in an excitement that seemed permanent

They were so ecstatic
I could go in among them, touch them, even break pieces off them
Pluck up flowers, without disturbing them in the least.
The birds simply flew wide, but were not for one moment distracted
From the performance of their feathers and eyes.
And the animals the same, though they avoided me
They did so with holy steps, and never paused
In the glow of fur which was their absolution in sanctity.

And their obedience, I could see that.

I could see I stood in a paradise of tremblings

At the crowded crossroads of all the heavens
The festival of all the religions

But a voice, a bell of cracked iron
Jarred in my skull

Summoning me to prayer

To eat flesh and to drink blood.

TED HUGHES

TWO HORSES

1

Earth heaved, splitting. Towers
Reared out. I emerged
Behind horses, updragging with oaken twists

Swaying castles of elastic

My fortifications moved on the sky
The ploughshare my visor

Crowned by wind burn, ploughing my kingdom

Instated by the sun's sway
The fortunes of war, a famished people
Corn barons.

2

I advanced
Under the November sooty gold heaven
Among angling gulls

Behind those earth-swaying buttocks
Their roil and gleam, as in a dark wind
And the smoky foliage of their labour
Their tree-strength

Hauling earth's betrothal
From an underworld, with crocus glints
A purplish cloak-flap
The click hooves flicking
Hot circles flashing back at me lightly

Bushy forest giants, gentle in harness
Their roots tearing and snapping

They were themselves the creaking boughs and the burden
Of earth's fleshiest ripeness, her damson tightest
Her sweetest

Earth splayed her thighs, she lay back.

3
The coulter slid effortless
The furrow's polished face, with a hiss
Coiling aside, a bow-wave that settled
Beside the poisonous brown river

I stumbled deeper.
             Hour after hour
The tall sweat-sleeked buttocks
Mill-wheels heavily revolving
Slackness to tautness, stretch and quiver—the vein-mapped
Watery quake-weight
In their slapping traces
             drawing me deeper

Into the muffled daze and toil of their flames
Their black tails slashing sideways
The occasional purring snort

The stubble's brassy whisper
The mineral raw earth smell, the town-wind of sulphur
The knotted worms, sheared by light
The everlasting war behind the shoulder
The old ploughman still young

Furrow by furrow darkening toward summer.

4
A shout—and the dream broke, against the thorns of the headland.
Chins back, backing

Trampling sideways, a jangling of brisk metals
High-kneed, levered by shouts
The plough hard over—

They had jerked awake
Into urgent seconds
Now they trod deep water, champing foam
Where were they suddenly?
            And suddenly they knew
Like turning in a bed, and settling to sleep
The share sank

With a hard sigh, the furrow-slice sprawled over

They bowed again to their worship.

5
The last friendly angels
Lifting their knees out of the earth, their clay-balled fetlocks
Heads down praying

And lifting me with them, into their furnace

I walked in their flames

Their long silk faces, shaggy as old sheepdogs
Their brown eyes, like prehistoric mothers
Their mouse-belly mouths, their spring-wire whiskers
Sudden yellow teeth of the nightmare and skull

Wading the earth's wealth
To soft horse-talk, nodding and slow in their power

Climbing the sky

On the crumbling edge.

Ted Hughes

PLACE NAMES

for Michael

You're building the fire, your face removed, distracted.
I watch you fill the clanking grill with flame and fan it,
coaxing smoke from coals. Remote, benched now on the sidelines,
I bide my time at the plank picnic table the park provides.
It's late August, and hot, though we're camped sky-high.
Sitting here, what I'm thinking about is several things:
a woman's place, for one, and what we'll name this baby,
and a breakfast we ate in a South Dakota cafe last summer.

There's some connection I can't quite place or name between
the baby I'm carrying and you cooking supper and me writing
poems and you and me camping by the Snake River. I guess
that unless you grew up east of Chicago, you can't imagine
the foreign charm of *Devil's Tower*, or the *Badlands*. I mean
what's Beirut, what's Helsinki, when there's *Cody, Wyoming,* or
Custer, South Dakota? We called my mother collect from there
and she, beside herself with excitement, her voice cracking,
cried to my father, "They're calling from *Custer, South Dakota!*"
They sold rocks there. You stole me a chip of rose quartz.
Later, at Craters of the Moon, you stole yourself a piece you
still prize, one holey lump of lava rock, two thousand years old.

This year we didn't go as far afield. A woman's place,
in my state, is close to home. We've pitched our tent
in the Blue Ridge, a far cry from the Big Horns. Now a
collect call would cost less and cause less excitement.
You're doing my work tonight, cooking supper while I think
about things: the price of bread, for instance, and the
distance between Virginia and Montana, and the way the baby
leaps when I start typing. There's some connection here
but I see it, sense it, only dimly. I look down at my calm
arms, tan, empty, idle, crossed at ease on the rough table.
You stir the stew and bring me bourbon in an enameled cup
and light a propane lamp, turning the sky a shade darker.

The cool dew is damp early now, a clue to September.
I rest my chin on my arms, wondering who we'll name
and where he'll fit in, and trying out tentatively
proper names: mother. Father. New places for us
to fit in, a new face to place, a third party who
might someday better name the smoky blue view we
share alone tonight, a pair of campers under a cone
of stars: two, and a new unknown camper coming up.

Kate Jennings

JOSEPH

Joseph, you were always in the background turning
red. Thumbs and fingers swollen from hammerslips,
the boss chuckling in the corner. Everything you made
blistered, when that angel came you bit
off part of your tongue. Found Mary at the well

wailing, swami right there in the dust. Mary,
you said off the bat, don't worry we don't
have to be that way. I'll build a roof
over your head, protect you from Roman fire,
floods and drought, name it.
Nights I'll lie at your feet, say Yes!

Well she'd seen the same angel, thought twice.
Then again. Why *not* let this funny man build a house?
Nice. Modest. Nothing quite fit. No door, but
this Arimathean at her feet, dreaming nails
and boards. Sandpaper! She needed a bed.

It didn't stop there, he built drawers
for her veils, cabinets for spices. One ladder
to climb on the roof, one for climbing down.

Then his breath on her ankles! She wrote
St. Anne, mother but he's close to my knees.
Please advise. The return post said About
time and Joseph built a clock in honor. Five minutes
fast. Mary threw up her hands at the dining room set.

Joseph, you're on the wrong side of the altar. Left.
Brides leave their bouquets by Mary, virgins
pray to her, not you. They don't want to step
over stools, go through a patron of basements. And attics.

Mary's got angels at her elbows, leaning over the baby,
double halo. You're by the ox, a hammer in your
belt, nails flashing wrong side out of that smile.

MARILYN JOHNSON

HENRY MANLEY, LIVING ALONE, KEEPS TIME

Sundowning,
the doctor calls it, the way
he loses words when the light fades.
The way the names of his dear ones
fall out of his eyeglass case.
Even under the face of his father
in an oval on the wall
he cannot say *Catherine, Vera, Paul,*
but goes on loving them out of place.
Window, wristwatch, cup, knife
are small prunes that drop from his pockets.
Terror sweeps him from room to room.
Knowing how much he weighed once
he knows how much has departed his life.
Especially he knows how the soul
can slip out of the body unannounced
like that helium-filled balloon
he opened his fingers on, years back.

Now it is dark. He undresses
and takes himself off to bed,
as loose in his skin as a puppy,
afraid the blankets will untuck,
afraid he will flap up, unblessed.
Instead, proper nouns return to his keeping.
The names of faces are put back
in his sleeping mouth. At first light
he gets up, grateful once more
for how coffee smells. Sits stiff
at the bruised porcelain table
saying them over, able
to with only the slightest catch:
Coffee, Coffee cup. Watch.

MAXINE KUMIN

SPLITTING WOOD AT SIX ABOVE

I open a tree.
In the stupefying cold
—ice on bare flesh a scald—
I seat the metal wedge
with a few left-handed swipes,
then with a change of grips
lean into the eight-pound sledge.

It's muslin overhead.
Snow falls as heavy as salt.
You are four months dead.
The beech log comes apart
like a chocolate nougat.
The wood speaks
first in the tiny voice
of a bird cry, a puppet-squeak,
and then all in a rush,
all in a passionate stammer.
The papery soul of the beech
released by wedge and hammer
flies back into air.

Times will do this as fair
to hickory, birch, black oak,
easing the insects in
till rot and freeze combine
to raise out of wormwood cracks,
blue and dainty, the souls.

They are thin as an eyelash.
They flap once, going up.

The air rings like a bell.
I breathe out drops—
cold morning ghost-puffs
like your old cigarette cough.
See you tomorrow, you said.
You lied.
We're far from finished! I'm still
talking to you (last night's dream);
we'll split the phone bill.
It's expensive calling
from the other side.

Even waking it seems
logical—
your small round
stubbornly airborne soul,
that sun-yellow daisy heart
slipping the noose of its pod,
scooting over the tightrope,
none the worse for its trip,
to arrive at the other side.

It is the sound
of your going I drive
into heartwood. I stack
my quartered cuts bark down,
open yellow-face up.

   Maxine Kumin

THE HOME PLACE

We never went anywhere.
We sat and listened to stew bubbling.
We sat and watched the skeins of darkness
unwind under bushes.
If we got up we got up to move the rocker
back a couple boards.
We never said anything.
If we said anything it was always
weather this and weather that.
Father would sit and think about it.
Mother would fold her hands
into her lap.
She was always getting ready to relax.
The wind blew.
But it never went anywhere.
It was always coming down
out of the west to beat against the house.
Nor did the house move.
Year after year it sat there fading
or letting its paint fall down like dandruff.
The wheat stayed out in the fields.
After it collapsed and rotted
the same tired birds got up
and flew into a clump of trees
to raise their young.
The dog barked at them then he died.
The cat came back from being lost.
Then disappeared.
Father said I think it'll rain.
And then it rained.

GREG KUZMA

SENTENCES

1

Water is condensing on the riffraff.
It is still only morning.
Silence breaks in the oak forest as the oaks wake.
There are a million words for it, one word.
Ice melts or stays, it is the same.
And in the tall high window thin Dorothy sits.
The book is good.
It is about goodbye.

Yesterday we signed and submitted various drafts.
The population coiled upon itself, seemed purified.
Murderers confessed on the avenues, but now,
now there is a darkness back again.
The books are blank, wherein we tried to see ourselves.
Music which used to delight shatters our ears.
The once and perfect eye discomforts.
Our room is plunged in gloom.

Still silence is inviolate.
It gives ground, it has to.
But the birds close down like teapots.
The mice find, at last, they are stricken.
Dumbstruck, the trees still and watch.
The moon's erect, and in the distance.
Father puts down his book in Italian.

We have begun to educate ourselves at last.
Life is a rumor, wildly distorted.
To be happy we must prepare for the worst.
And it comes on reared hind legs.
It lays its paw across our dinner napkin.
Its accents blow all day back and forth in the yard.
Tonight we will speak of what ails us.
And purified, sleep a half sleep.
We have ached long enough, is it not so?

The mountain, above us, is blue.
And you, dear one, how you are dying to be good.
It was in you from the first.
Perhaps you will have your chance.
Though now it is snowing and the sky is black.

Music from a distant room.
How do we begin to dance or to resist it.

2

John is at college, working his sums.
The cat crawls over the lampshade, sits on your lap.
Night smuggles dark shapes past your window.
In the morning the yard seems empty, or more full.
John is the scholarship student.

It is dark where you are.
Night falls.
It falls deeper.
You light a cigarette.

3

You are very much alone and it is good.
You are empty like a dish the cat has finished.
You feel put down by everything.
You almost cannot move in a straight line.
You do not believe in anything.
Your life is falling apart.
What was there ever there in the first place.

There is a story to it, and you know how it goes.
It has gone on a long time, but now it is nearly over.
Though it gets better at the end.
You know it by heart, you have known it so long.
It reassures you, you turn the pages.
It bores you, you turn the pages.
Sometimes it seems it is there in the book and no more.
Other times you are the principal character.
And every one is chasing you.

We can start with the flesh.
We can work backward.
There is slime in us that is primitive.
The composition of our blood where fish swim.
What good does it do.

You say you are going away.
They have started the car and brought it around front.
Your scarf blows in the wind.
It is starting to rain.
It shatters your smile in the driveway.

4

How I go on and on.
It is incredible, this sky.
Children rush by in the street.
The front of the paper is covered with bad news.
Demons will feast on your bones, or have already.
We are serene, we have been to the dark lands.
We suffer the banishment, we have our TVs.
The day is a ladder, we leave it leaning against the house.
Birds sit on the rungs where we will never climb.

No, we have reached the rooftops.
We look down.
What a breathless view.
Our chests heave.
We do not have the courage to jump.
We are afraid that people will think we are in great pain.
All this shows how bad off we are.
But look at the view, the rooftops around us.
So this is what the cat sees hungry for the kill.

GREG KUZMA

EVERY WOMAN YOU LOVED

for Alan Crawley, 1887-1975

Every woman you loved
I am
but I am the only one left
now to come

At the hospital bed
I stand beside your spare form
stooping over
to kiss the bent brow
to hear you say
from your blind, deaf world
"Oh do not go away—
Stay. Stay!"

I seek for your palm
the grasp is firm
free and happy as always
pulsing, cogent
but no flesh there
nothing but its end,
bare bone—despair
earth's sufferance—
O my dear
        my dear

How can we ever connect
the disappearing flesh
collapsing bone
with belief in the heart's everness
endlessly beating
its way home?

        DOROTHY LIVESAY

VISION

"Vision," we said, hearing how things turned out
    Just as the sage predicted; "no mere guess:
He could see through appearances and probe
    Deep to those roots from which our future springs."

"I had a vision," he said; "an angel stood
    Before me in a blaze of light; a mouth
Close to my face breathed in my ear, whispered
    'The New Jerusalem'—and I woke up."

But one, stripped of half an eye's vision,
    Says "Lord, let me keep what's left, to enjoy
The light of common day; spare my first sight,
    And you can keep foresight and second sight."

                        EDWARD LOWBURY

SHARKS AT THE NEW YORK AQUARIUM

Suddenly drawn through the thick glass plate
And swimming among them, I imagine
Myself as, briefly, part of the pattern
Traced in the water as they circulate
Endlessly, obeying the few laws
That thread the needle of their simple lives:
One moment in a window of serrated knives,
Old-fashioned razors and electric saws.
And then the sudden, steep, sidewinding pass:
No sound at all. The waters turning pink,
Then rose, then red, after a long while clear.
And here I am again, outside the tank,
Uneasily wrapped in our atmosphere!
Children almost never tap on the glass.

                    CHARLES MARTIN

FAIRY TALE OF AN
OLD FASHIONED DAUGHTER

More than once she'd laid down her law
for daughters and mothers:
"We must establish boundaries like nations,
draw maps of our territories
(your river, my mountain),
place armed guards at the bridges
and highway checkpoints
and issue passports."

But when her mother was suddenly dead
she could not plunder her house,
strip the rooms of Orientals,
cherry four posters and loveseats,
and pack the booty back to her territory.

She knew she was crazy
but she moved into her mother
and took up her life
like a piece of needlework.
She crocheted her way into the church
and asked the jangling bracelets
and the permanent waves over
for bourbon and a bite to eat.

She was the model of decorum.
She cashed the royalty checks
for her mother's childrens stories,
painted still-lifes of flowers and fruit,
wrote doggerel for her friends
and nibbled cookies after lunch.

When she wanted to scream
she napped instead
or drew her shades
and drank like a woman at war.
She imagined a man in overalls
with a hairy chest and massive arms
who chased her nude through the house.
She saw herself spinning
lovely and warm from room to room.
But she had grown to fit her mother's dresses.
No one would want her.

One night she had a dream of hands.
They followed her through the rooms
latching the windows, locking the doors.
They shut her in darkness.
She turned on them. They grabbed her.
She pried at the fingers.
Her wrists twisted so tight
her shoulder blades turned upside down
and her elbows wept.

She woke and knew
the hands were her own.
In the morning light she watched them
make the bed and butter the toast,
while her mother's intricate cats
guarded her house
like Egyptians.

MOLLY McKAUGHAN

"...IN MANY BODIES."

I am, shall be, the rock; I was the seed;
    shall be, and was and still both fire and clay.
I am, shall be the earthquake, was the ice;
    shall be, and was, and ever, light of day.
I am and shall be starlight, gossamer;
    shall be red honey, was and shall be wax.
I am and shall be lilies, was the lake;
    all tides that laboured countless Doomsdays' cracks.

I am the thought of relativity,
    one indeterminate of time and space.
I am, and am not, Nature, partly veiled;
    incarnate now for crisis of the race
I am my consciousness, sample of man;
    inhabit galaxies, yet home in Greece.
I am both dying year, concurrent Spring;
    diversity and oneness, tension, peace.

One and at one with all that breathes and lives,
    I am, this darkened solstice, Christ's Mass Eve,
Hands clasped with you—poets whose friendship gives
    "I am" live worth—unseparated, whole.

One and at one, our nearly two-score band
    shall be, and is, bold pattern; each may be
Unique, contributory. All exemplar stand
    as unity of caring, "As one soul..."

                        HUGH McKINLEY

ST. VINCENT'S

Thinking of rain clouds that rose over the city
on the first of the year

in the same month
I consider that I have lived daily and with
eyes open and ears to hear
these years across from St. Vincent's Hospital
above whose roof those clouds rose

its bricks by day a French red under
cross facing south
blown-up neoclassic façades the tall
dark openings between columns at
the dawn of history
exploded into many windows
in a mortised face

inside it the ambulances have unloaded
after sirens' howling nearer through traffic on
Seventh Avenue long
ago I learned not to hear them
even when the sirens stop

they turn to back in
few passersby stay to look
and neither do I

at night two long blue
windows and one short one on the top floor
burn all night
many nights when most of the others are out
on what floor do they have
anything

I have seen the building drift moonlit through geraniums
late at night when trucks were few
moon just past the full
upper windows parts of the sky
as long as I looked
I watched it at Christmas and New Year
early in the morning I have seen the nurses ray out through
arterial streets
in the evening have noticed internes blocks away
on doorsteps one foot in the door

I have come upon the men in gloves taking out
the garbage at all hours
piling up mountains of
plastic bags white strata with green intermingled and
black
I have seen the pile
catch fire and studied the cloud
at the ends of the jets of the hoses
the fire engines as near as that
red beacons and
machine-throb heard by the whole body

I have noticed molded containers stacked outside
a delivery entrance on Twelfth Street
whether meals from a meal factory made up with those
mummified for long journeys by plane
or specimens for laboratory
examination sealed at the prescribed temperatures
either way closed delivery

and approached faces staring from above
crutches or tubular clamps
out for tentative walks
have paused for turtling wheelchairs
heard visitors talking in wind on each corner
while the lights changed and
hot dogs were handed over at the curb

in the middle of afternoon
mustard ketchup onions and relish
and police smelling of ether and laundry
were going back

and I have known them all less than the papers of our days
smoke rises from the chimneys do they have an incinerator
what for
how warm do they believe they have to maintain the air
in there
several of the windows appear
to be made of tin
but it may be the light reflected
I have imagined bees coming and going
on those sills though I have never seen them

who was St. Vincent

W. S. Merwin

FOR JULIA, IN THE DEEP WATER

The instructor we hire
Because she does not love you
Leads you into deep water,
The deep end
Where the water is darker.
Her open, encouraging arms
That never get nearer
Are merciless for your sake.

You will dream this water always
Where nothing draws nearer.
Wasting your valuable breath
You will scream for your mother—
Only your mother is drowning
Forever in the thin air
Down at the deep end.
She is doing nothing,
She never did anything harder.
And I am beside her.

I am beside her
In this imagination.
We are waiting
Where the water is darker.
You are over your head.
Screaming, you are learning
Your way toward us,
You are learning how
In the helpless water
It is with our skill
We live in what kills us.

JOHN N. MORRIS

ASPECTS OF LILAC

By the turn of the driveway, two lilacs have called
Attention to themselves, not by an excess
Of bloom but by an attenuation
Of design: altered shadow on gravel.
Gone for good are those understated
Cases I rescued from worthless soil:
Ripped-off dusty miller from the beach,
Or, struck by overdoses of rain,
Spoiled spotted-leaf geranium. Worse
Is the thud of birds that kill themselves
By flinging their bodies with force against
Glass windows and doors as if this were
Some sort of morgue for feathered things.
The deaf and dumb would find all language
Futile here; nature is silent—
But underneath the silence, struggle.
While powder-puff clouds are showing off
Quickening shapes against more stately
Clouds behind them, an ant has dragged
A fly across the threshold, a mealy
Bug fastened its sticky jaws
Into the crotch of two green stems,
Chewing the asparagus fern to scruff.
Last night the moon had a Byzantine flare
Of lemon gold like the gold-leaf halos
One sees in the early Italian Masters—
Venice, in fact, comes to mind, the palazzos'
Sandcastle, ice-cream feats, effects
Childish but pleasing, of spun-stone heights,
While a rat stands gnawing a lettuce leaf
At the edge of one of the canals. And sex
Like a frog jumps onto the screen at once,

Its spiritual and degraded aspects
Equally keen. In fall, when the first
Earth colors harden and oak fire starts
Its flame and rust, memory dotes
On the old clichés of the unexpected.
Desire never knows the end of the book
Any more than the leaves of the lilac dug
Up in the woods, brought home, and planted
Can tell us whether its roots next spring
Will burst into purple or white cascades.

                        HOWARD MOSS

NOTES FROM THE CASTLE

The sunlight was not our concern or even
The pane it shone through, and no one was going
Down for the mail, and the four lettuces
The gardener brought as a gift seemed to be
A calculated bounty, so that early on
We knew we were going to be stuck with ourselves
The rest of the day, the vicissitudes
Marching in rows from the forest, the balms
Not arriving till nightfall. On the prowl
Since morning, the wind had a touch too much
Of motivation, an annoying way
Of exactly ruffling the same oak leaf
As if it were practicing a piano trill;
All day, repetitive birds, far off,
Were either boring themselves to death
Or, drunk on instinct, doing their thing:
Ritual dances, territorial rites—
The whole imperial egg. What nests
Ambition is weaving in us is hard
To say: After the flat occasion,
The unshared sphere, what childish wish
Doesn't grow hopeless faced by the unnatural?
And all the recommended cures are useless:
A cheery hello to the disaffected
At breakfast? A soupful of tears at dinner?
You could spill the whole silly story out
To one more demanding, ill-tempered beauty
Who happened to cross your path in the aisle
Of the cereal section of the A. & P.,
And still every greedy shopping cart,
First overstuffed and then abandoned
In the parking lot, would leave in its wake
Some human need, ignored, half starved . . .

Torn between having nothing to say
And saying it, whole diaries get down:
How terrible to have dressed beautifully for the rain! . . .
I was launched on New York's bisexual muddle . . .
And so on. And always the hoped-for redeemer
Turns up and turns with a country stare:
The girl in the lime linen shorts, the boy
With blond corn-silk tow hair, the heart
Speeding up until they speak: the dross
Of cars, the sportsman's life, and money;
And so, believing that you had come
To rest among the innocent soldiers
Of sleep, you had merely stumbled on
Another temporary battlefield
As never-lasting as the shine of water.

HOWARD MOSS

NEW ENGLAND LANDSCAPE

Walking the shore
On a blue and yellow day,
I try to imagine
What was there
Before the ship,
Loaded with religion,
Stopped in the bay
And turned the place
Into a cornfield.
What I mean
Are the vines like boas,
Jays and orioles
Bright as parrots,
Green trees crowding
From hill to hill.

And I try to understand
The way it looked
Through the travelers' eyes
As they jumped or rowed
Through the knife-tip waves
To the shelving sand—
How they must have stared,
And measured their courage,
Where the black oaks puffed
In the powdery snow,
And hawks slid over,
And moose swam through
With antlers like wings!

And, viewing the smooth
Civilized horizons,
I feel the wound—
The shiver of bedrock,
The hook in the glittering
Marshes and sand
And the mute damp trees
And the sun-warmed stone—
How they prospered and shone
To the very edge
Of that cold morning
When, without warning,
The little ship lay
In the throat of the bay
Like a bone.

        MARY OLIVER

POEM FOR MY FATHER'S GHOST

Now is my father
A traveler, like all the bold men
He talked of, endlessly
And with boundless admiration,
Over the supper table,
Or gazing up from his white pillow—
Book on his lap always, until
Even that grew too heavy to hold.

Now is my father free of all binding fevers.
Now is my father
Traveling where there is no road.

Finally, he could not lift a hand
To cover his eyes.
Now he climbs to the eye of the river,
He strides through the Dakotas,
He disappears into the mountains. And though he looks
Cold and hungry as any man
At the end of a questing season,

He is one of *them* now:
He cannot be stopped.

Now is my father
Walking the wind,
Sniffing the deep Pacific
That begins at the end of the world.

Vanished from us utterly,
Now is my father circling the deepest forest—
Then turning in to the last red campfire burning
In the final hills,

Where chieftains, warriors and heroes
Rise and make him welcome,
Recognizing, under the shambles of his body,
A brother who has walked his thousand miles.

Mary Oliver

THE EXPLORERS

Caressing each other's bodies, rapt explorers
of dearly known terrain—the slope of shoulders,
the long curve of the back, with its minute valley,
its cloudy rising hills—hands delighting
in the sleek glide of the skin, muscled ridges
drawn taut, the clean profile of the bones—
ready for love, past ready for love, but on,
on go those hands, lost in their own volitions,
in a delirium of touch, like dancers moving
in an empty ballroom after the music's through,
as if some memory were being verified,
some blind man's landscape traced, some lost map drawn—
as if these surrendering bodies under these deft, warm
hands were melting—melting—melting like things of snow.

PAUL PETRIE

IMMERSION

When the Hardshell Baptists led their cowering
sons and daughters to the river for Immersion,
we dry-land Methodists came along to count the drownings.
Whoever thought that risk attends redemption?
Pajama-clad and barefoot, looking shrunken,
my schoolfriends, culprits all, stepped off the bank
to martyrdom as the preacher standing hip-deep
in the current like a bridge-pier
called out each not-yet-Christian name.
I gaped to see him take my best friend Harold
by the wrist and then the head, and palm
him under the way you'd drown a pony,
his other hand held up I guess to Heaven
while he shouted *I baptise thee* and so on,
each word a fatal lungful. When Harold
broke water he snorted like a walrus
and tottered blindly back to land amen.
Safe there in my dry skin, how I envied him!—
my friend, who had stepped once into a river
and bravely held his breath until God noticed
and now stood chilled
and chattering with salvation
on the altering shore.

Jarold Ramsey

MY TWELVE GODCHILDREN

My twelve godchildren stood before me saying

> What were the vows you said over us
> When you held us at the font
> In our christening dress of lawn and lace?

I stood before my twelve godchildren saying

> When on the day the black sky will brandish the white pen
> When six of you are ten,
> Reach for it.
>
> When you have gone some leagues you will come upon
> Three crows uttering 'cras.'
> With your left hand, point at them.
>
> Consider what you may make live:
> The laurel, olive, ash.
>
> Do not hunt for badges. They tear the shirt finally.
>
> Do not, three of you, hunt for symbols in refuse.

My twelve godchildren stood before me asking

> Shall we bind our plaits together?
>
> When the prisoners are barred from entering the prison,
> Shall we lead them in?
>
> If the figure in the corner speaks, shall we speak to it?
>
> Shall we have the peacocks come down two by two?

I stood before my godchildren saying

> Leave five of the seven-colored leaves of autumn
> Behind you before you go to fell timber
> In the imperial forests.
>
> Against the bells calling the faithful
> Close your ears, especially in foreign cities.
>
> When there be nine of you waylost and keening
> Go for exile on the prow-breaking sea.

My twelve godchildren stood before me crying

> Why, when you teach us windsongs
> May we not lie down where the winter wind is stabled?
> Why, when you teach us warsongs
> Do you not arm us with shields the weight of five seas?

I stood before my twelve godchildren saying

> God has inscribed in the core of the earth
> In cataracts of gold not yet discovered
> Four elegies to fulfil prophecies
> That none of the twelve of you will see
>
> But He has most surely written them.

My twelve godchildren stood before me crying

> But what shall we do, for we have seen from the promontory
> Proceeding westward over bridges, the caravans?
>
> In our hearts' lovely chambers has sleep set in.
> Must death follow?
>
> What shall we do, after the eagles have gone?
> What shall we, after the eagles?

I stood before my twelve godchildren saying

> Beneath him the cliff gives way to the ravine below,
> Death trumpets the King Elephant through canyoned space
> Holding in his trunk the orb and sceptre.
>
> Listen, when the stories of his death come back to you.

PRISCILLA STEWART RANDOLPH

THE ANCESTORS AND WHAT THEY LEFT

There's a mouse in the fir tree,
a thousand planets spinning off center....

On the earth's thin crust, a thread, a residue.
Some of the dead rising to the surface.
My great uncle and my aunt, grandfather
putting on his shoe. There's the hull
of the boat that brought him here, now a fist
of coal. Grandmother left her scent
on the doorknob, a voiceprint in the air.

What we used to call debris now helps us
breathe: this tree's leaves
contain my father's veins, its steam a reminiscence
of his breath. Who needs the dead to speak
when they leave their signals everywhere?

This loneliness will pass, this feeling
off center. In a moment you'll leave the room
of this world and not return. What doors
have not been opened, what more could we ask for?

On my hand there's a line which extends
beyond my life, its love and fame: it's a chain,
a leash that ties me to my past.
It's irrevocable: I'm on the dock, waving
to the Jews I am, disguised as bureaucrats
with secretaries I love, officials I can't stand.

Before that on the farm, the vodka and potatoes,
I carry their sprout and smell. And the pastoral
sense of the salt lick, the tremor, cows
kneeling on a hill. Underneath, in the damp
graveyard that extends from the earth's surface
to its core, someone's father whispering,
I'm pushing through the dust that I've become

And in my head I hear his longing and his call.
We're like two figures touching
in a mirror, a trick to find out which is us.
And if I light a candle, pass my palm above the flame,
the smudge that's left—that dark streak, that film—
becomes my sign, the hillside of my own terrain.

IRA SADOFF

VISITING THE MATERNITY HOSPITAL

Now I am one of the visitors;
Middle-aged, an intruder in outdoor clothes,
Watching the tiny, yawling babies through the glass,
Mouthing outside the camaraderie
Echoes of a cold and grimy chaos,
Hidden behind these shining double windows.

The nurses have changed,
But I remember this ward,
Where two-day bouts with pain,
Caesarians, breech-presentations, stitches
Were calmly knitted into a tidy pattern
Between our morning tea and the early feed.

Each left and returned on a trolley
To find, alone, a body that obeyed
Old, deep-lying forces which broke
The law and order of the will
In earth-quake shocks
And threw-up life in a tidal wave of muck
To cast the long-nursed dream
On the heart's beach.
Then the unforgettable, unforgotten
Was briskly tucked into place
Behind the jokes and writing of letters,
And setting of hair.

At three-o'clock the visitors came,
Mothers of unimagined teen-age sons,
Borne on a tide of clamourous worry and need
Which spent itself about our solid peace,
And died, with claims of past and future time,
Under our sweet absorption in the now.

MARGARET SCOTT

MAN INTO BILLIARD BALL

He was all angles, sharp as a knife,
and when, maliciously, we said:
"you'll end like us, compromising with life,"
he stuck razor blades in his smile
and chopped himself down to the bone.

He reckoned he was ivory clear through,
a sort of human dice that rolled straight sevens
by evading formulating fingers,
considering brows.

But the knocks got him, as we said they would:
it was all click clack and clippety,
there was no roll, no cushion to spin back from,
no pocket to fall into after a long white run.

So, "Make me a billiard ball" he prayed;
and we did: buffed off his chips with honey
and basted him with putty.
Such rosy ladyfingers rolled him round
he soon forgot where butter ended
and the guns began.

He was all one, circular, smooth, comfy.
The ladyfingers cooled themselves in money,
became ten white icicles moving easily
over quiescent belly: chilled him to porcelain,
blind, opaque and hard. He could see neither out nor in.

He'll run where you want him now.
For Christ's sake keep him moving,
delude him with a sense of purpose.
Intensify his love of cushions.
Whisper immortal ease into prosaic pockets.

Prepare him for another death.

GRAHAM SEAL

A MAN AND HIS WATCH

1

Awake too early, even before false dawn,
he heard its tick from where he'd laid it down.
The webs of sleep still hung in bleary tatters;
he could see nothing in the room except
off to the left, at rest on edge, that dial
whose luminous darts endured their endless ambit.
The tick fell heavier than it did by day,
more adamant or more admonitory,
as if a dark spell might intensify
the burden of its rhythmless recital.
But there was only the absence of other sound
to thank for that. He recalled a warm afternoon
when after an hour of making love that seemed
perfect as flesh could hope to bestow or be blessed with
he lay back with his arm over his eyes
and heard it about its business on the bureau:
loud then too, though the room was filled with light.

2

At 8:23 one morning it stopped dead.
Shaking it, rapping it on a table top
roused no reaction. It was almost indecently
self-conscious of an artifact, he thought,
to witness by its ultimate, mute expression
to the true moment of its own demise.
The hands, hung in a fixed and helpless V,
pointed apparently past their own tight compass
toward some far termini off the cosmic schedule.
He took it to a taciturn Swede whose fingers,
given a shift in superintending will,
could have made a career of cracking safes.
A spring and a bit of cleaning did the trick,
restored a world of order to his wrist,
the comfort of keeping tabs on wasted time.

3
These were anomalies. Typically its behavior
has been to abide an unobtrusive servant.
An uncle, elderly, who'd never married,
died and left him a whole houseful of clocks.
All of them ran, and not a one kept pace
with any other. Two minutes each side of an hour
loosed a barrage of bongs and cuckoo-hoots.
It was like living with a German band.
He sold the lot, and bought himself the watch
herein referred to, wonderfully less abrasive
a token of mortality, he reasoned:
no up-to-the-minute news you didn't ask for.
And so it goes—or so they go together,
meeting appointments. Moving his arm he winds
this diligent disc, forgotten till consulted,
taking perpetual measure of the pulse
its platinum links luxuriously surround.
A half-handcuff. And only very lately
has he begun to feel its intimate weight.

Robert B. Shaw

TO MARKET, TO MARKET

for MCP

She couldn't (or could she?)
Live with the three chins,
The mouth that took the world
To its plush accordion,
Dutch seas of gravy, cigar
Angling, the *Titanic*'s last stack
Above its foundering hulk.

His hands over the omelette were
Immaculate, the nails' white
Quarter moons dancing, while one
Big opal seemed to feast its eye
On her through the coffee, mints,
And velvet gastronomic sigh.
(She resolved she couldn't!)

Pushing the table back, he was
Atlas shrugging off the world,
Napoleon rolling it toward the stars—
So complete his every gesture.
How odd, she laughed, all this!
The man was obscene, selfish.
Smiling, his wet lips pursed

To a primrose. Yet, squeezing into
Cabs, puffing up red-carpeted stairs,
He courted her, she let herself
Be courted, those two jowls hemispheres
Into which all fell to the left
Or right. A diamond big as a parfait,
He said, his red tongue winking.

Rice salted down the two of them
In the dark car that glided home
To the earthquake of his bed,
Where, for a moment, the sweet terror
Stalked her—rabbit in a white field—before
The sun fell on her and the moon and, oh,
She danced above the seas a light rain!
And, tasted, drunk, folded to the earth,
Slept quiet as his rib again.

     Robert Siegel

BACK RIVER WINTER

For some good time I mourned you only in walking
through heat-haze and the fat proud wild-flowers
where the fireflies waited for us to run.

But in winter which is infinitely young
with a rumpled white sheet that invites all
cessation to the tumbling pain in the nerves?

There are apples in the yard, red and soft.
Who would ask why they fell? What they say, buried
in their dark skins, their seeds more perfect than reason,

is less inaudible than weeping. I have some need
to speak of final things in my own tongue, perimeters
I must keep to like the cautious wheeling fishhawk

who eats the apples in bad times. Today in snow
I watched them peel a man from his tree-clenched car.
I saw the wrecker slide with its prize, go away

like a fat woman, like you, a kind of jolly dance
turned sour that with one finger I could blot out.
Then was gone. Was snow. Was mud bridging its wound

and not even a bluejay to break that vision. Yet
I did walk out by the river cheerfully feathering
the same sun I could pretend was my daughter's hair,

and in pines knotting up odd shadows, believe it
or not, I could imagine I heard the promised Christ
beautifully breathing that dead man's name.

Tonight someone in the cold will ask as I ask,
what is the trick of it? In this weather I think
I must learn how to walk out of despair, to see

what the apples fall into is a place without answer
or asking, and accept it as the fishhawk does, the man
who drives the wrecker and sings a song of one

woman he has not loved for the whole of a single night.
I must give over grief and begin in the winter
I love to love whatever believes in the good.

And if you should find me whistling your old fame
among great-grandchildren, remember it is what
you have taught me, and nothing less will I know.

        DAVE SMITH

SOME MARVELOUS QUARRY

He, walking home from school,
Saw something that looked like a hole
In the February swamp's blurred shoals
Of thawing ice and freezing pools.
And because he had to see what it was
He leapt and slid and fell on bars
Of ice until at last he lay out flat,
His face only a foot
From the mound of a porcupine caught
In the arms of a going and coming winter.
No quill stirred in the wind. The unwary
Eyes gleamed as though fixed on some marvelous quarry.
Had there been stench, he'd have known
It as the stench of death. Had there been
Maggots pumping in their cylinders
Of greed he'd have known it as
The death he knew. But this was changeless,
Perfected, the unmoving shadow of everything
That moves.
             At home, of course, he had
To be punished for clothes muddy and wet,
For books spoiled. But since he was one who easily wept,
Even for soft rebukes, his father only played,
Half-smiling, at bringing down the limp belt
On his outstretched hands.
The boy paled but could make no tears.
They looked then, father and son,
At each other with separate fears.
They guessed much, but neither could bear
To believe no punishment would make the boy
Flinch and cry and forget what he now knew.

                                    RADCLIFFE SQUIRES

ELEGY FOR AGATHA CHRISTIE

In the pantry, a decanter reflects
Topaz pools on pastries and tins
As the late sun flows in through an open window.
Outside, a tall woman bends and clips off
Red roses for a perfect setting, the guests'
First meeting. That picturesque,
Elegant dinner will be disturbed by which

Person's memory of an incident in Egypt?
The butler yawns behind the door, pauses
Before crossing the hall, and hears
The guests rising from their chairs.
The sticky mark above an ear
Locks every door that night. Upstairs,
A girl in a flowered dress holds a photograph
And weeps; the man in the corridor

Makes a fist at his own image in the glass,
And all over the world
People sit up, not wanting to finish, and still
Not able to sleep. They think they know,
Knowing themselves!

Now one woman is missed as our lost hours
Are not. For us she killed the individual,
Evil people, and the hours. Characters
For results. They are not
Ourselves or even like
The crystals of our hatred and distrust.

The airs of a murder clearing up,
And the lost hours
That saved us for the accomplishment of sleep—
We are grateful for the murders, and we know
That all she killed for us has, now, killed her:

Time and boredom, preparing us for the rest
That's dark and formal,
Like the butler sleeping in a chair, his large
Hands innocently folded between his knees.
             PAMELA STEWART

A CLICHÉ POEM FOR YOUR LEAVING

Last things first.
I would not by the hair of my chin
utter a word against you
except to ask where in hell
is the silver lining.

No news is not necessarily

says the philosopher, pleased
with himself, his head buried,
and as always, just enough off
the mark of the real world
to appear as wise as he is old.

I hope to God

I don't pass this way again.
As it is the best place to end
was at the beginning
as it were.
For the time being

holding the short end of the stick

I mean to contemplate
only until six of one
seems once more
half a dozen.
I am well, also alive.

It's just a matter of time
until the truth
will out.
Till then, I am resigned
in name only and, as before

left to my own devices.

JOHN STONE

SWEATER

It doesn't matter if the light fails.
Tonight, my fingers move automatically
Along the rows, each stitch
As familiar as a bead of the rosary.

I simply follow the family pattern
My Irish grandmothers knit into sweaters
For their sons, the fine threads
Spun off the skulls of Nordic sailors.

And when I stop and raise my hands,
It will be in the way of a priest
Blessing boats. I'll poke my arms
Through the dark and listen

For the clack of needles, oars.
I'll prostrate myself on the floor,
Let down the nets, the great
Walls of the house, and float out,

The tides, the full moon, a tangle
Of yarn, pulling me in, cell by cell,
My flesh unravelling, all revealing
Marks gone: scars, face, fingerprints,

My whole body the shore by dawn.

MARY SWANDER

THE GOING AWAY OF YOUNG PEOPLE

1

This was the day
The crumbs from last night's dinner
Lay all day on the table.

Your room filled only by sunlight
Is darkened by the late sleeper.

        You forgot your love.
        I'd mail it but
        There's the chore of string
        And paper and
The timbre of hi-fi turned off
Strings the psyche.
        Anyway it's stuff I'm used
        To stumbling over in various
        Recesses of my house
        Wondering why I haven't
        Given it away, put it
        To some use—
        But keep on hoarding it, ashamed.

2

And our sailers-away hang yet full sail
In our autumn windows,
The windows across the street
Becalmed of young people.
Grass infiltrates their marigolds.
The garage cries out.

3

I won't say goodbye.
But all leave-taking is a permanence.
We can't be sewed back up.
My mother's face at the window
Like a postage stamp
Hinges a faded September.

4

And over a drink my old friend fights tears,
Fights impatiently sympathy,
At her window cuts at the traffic
With her hand—"It was all woods!
Gone! And I've failed, too."

5

Windows between Septembers,
More and more windows,
Muffling, fogging over,
At last reflect only me
In car window, kitchen window,
Across-the-street windows,
This window I open over your bed
In case you should come back
For what you forgot.

ELEANOR ROSS TAYLOR

MACDUFF

This wet sack, wavering slackness
    They drew out silent through the long
Blood-edged incision, this black
    Unbreathing thing they must first
Hoist from a beam by its heels and swing
    To see whether it could yet expel
Death through each slimy nostril,
    This despaired-of, half-born mishap
Shuddered into a live calf, knew
    At a glance mother, udder and what it must do
Next and did it, mouthing for milk.
    The cow, too, her womb stitched back inside,
Her hide laced up, leans down untaught
    To lick clean her untimely firstborn :
"Pity it's a male." She looms there innocent
    That words have meanings, but long ago
This blunt lapsarian instinct, poetry,
    Found life's sharpest, readiest
Rhyme, unhesitating—it was knife—
    By some farm-yard gate, perhaps,
That led back from nature into history.

              CHARLES TOMLINSON

SALMON FISHING

At six I learned the salmon,
one early August morning after father had shut off the motor
and taken up the lines in his rough hands,
letting them spread out slowly in the water;
all around us the hooks glittered through the fog
as he spoke softly, saying how the salmon were going
back to the first rivers they had ever known,
fresh water, leaving the sea.
And when he pulled that first bunch in,
all I could see were the thick jagged teeth,
the upper jaw curving like a hook over the lower.
Years later he told me how it was all for death,
for the lifetime of sperm they could pump out,
each aiming at some thousand eggs in a hollowed sand grave.
But at six I could only watch them slap against the bottom of the boat
and wonder if I would ever be able to find my way home alone.

On this hot August night I tell some new lover about the salmon;
I turn back over and sort through all the old Augusts,
try to recall your face, father, your boat a black spot on the horizon,
try to count off how many of our quarrels still have blood left in them.
It is all that's left I am afraid of,
afraid that on some dark night when this new man reaches for me
I will feel the heavy salt air flood through me
and see in the shadows an old man's hands spreading the lines
and I will roll back from the lover's touch
and curl into myself, guilty and alone.
After 24 years, that much of you implanted in me.

NANCE VAN WINCKEL

HER DREAM

She breathes, lying flat in the night, catches her breath
And holds it, starting, stopping, suddenly turning
To the wall, to the ceiling for their coldest comfort,
Lets out all breath as if done with it,
Then after a dead moment, after the hours
Of wrestling with her pain, she begins deep, steady breathing.

I lie beside her, listening
And staring at the clenched hands of the clock, counting
A prayer to the God of Numbers to lead her
Down out of harm, to healing within healing
Without me, even without herself to follow
Into darkness softer than her pillow.

She breathes more deeply. I catch myself
Napping, then snap awake. The clock is in gauze. Her breath
Comes quick and shallow
With the sudden abrupt pauses of a dreamer,
The muffled laughter and whimpers from the other room of her sleep,
From the lurching corridor, the sinking stairwell,

And I turn to her and follow her
And blunder into her dream where the cackling women
Claw with their broken nails, where the hooded, berserk warlocks
Slash at us both in vain, where the mad dwarves can't betray us,
Where we float through the wreckage of our shadows,
Breathing till morning.

DAVID WAGONER

MIDSUMMER, ENGLAND

At Henley, the sky-blue striped pavilions
are boathouses, the royal river
beer-bottle green with broken lights,
the legendary landscapes are alive,
palpable air: woods, castles, manors, suns,
pressing their postcards on you as you drive.

Great summer takes its ease,
ankling the shallows, cloudy dresses bloat
and cling clearly round the women's knees
as Christ harangues the indifferent from his boat
by Cookham's river.

Riots of color in the Supplements,
startling bright mustard squares
flare tropically amid
fields trimmed by centuries of reticence;
midsummer's broad abandon will subside
like hills rolling in heat waves; what will not
is the fear of darkness entering England's vein,
the noble monuments spat on by rain,
the imperial blood corrupted, the dark tide.

But summer persists through the pain,
it forces the leaf
and tries, through love-nourishing rain,
to dissolve individual grief,
history, and heartbreak.

Prodigious summer whose black fruit includes—
past this and that great house,
between hills bracketing thunder—
a great cloud's shadow that grows close
as the past, a chill that intrudes
under the heat, under the centuries,
rooks swinging in the wind under great boughs,
lynched crows on a green field.

What hurts most is to think that I was healed.

DEREK WALCOTT

INSTALLING THE BEES

First this: a thousand bees
balled up in one black heart,
a loud wind, a fist of heat,
locked in their thin cage,
edgy with energy.

You carry them out to the hive,
gently, their delicate balance
locked in your dangerous hands,
gorged with your sweet words,
the sky buzzing with dusk.

Then this: the hive like a white thumb
stump on the frozen land.
You open it slowly
and pour the bees out,
as if an escarpment, a sluice.

Now the bees seethe and roil.
You slap down the cover, suddenly
frightened at the weight
that falls from your arms,
the splash of dark waters.

You lift your white hands
to your eyes, waxen, honeyed,
pale lilies, mums, the dead man's
flowers, a thousand bees buzzing
in your wrists.

     RONALD WALLACE

FROM THE OTHER COUNTRY

But you do not consider how long I have lived in this country.
Its skies move through my skull, and the changing light
over the water; like whales the humped mountains
surface in my dreams, and never were trees
thwart like these in flight from the salt harsh gales.

The customs of the people, it is true,
are not mine; in farms and one-street towns
they enact strict rituals of thrift, worship, pleasure.
Lights burn late where slow accounts are reckoned,
the drunk crashes prone in dying embers,

and beneath tribal tokens, ancient recitations.
Often indeed through main street and glen
drums throb savage annunciation, the door
opens to a rain of bullets, car-lights pick out
the corpse in a ditch. "It's a madness going on,"

they say. Did you think madness so dull?
Look: how finite among the weltering green
these settlements, no margins to nourish the odd.
Knowing their place, they grow, pray, wed, kill, die.
Even their knowing smiles have a terrible innocence

which you do not understand. Nor, though you hear,
how their soft gutturals and singing intonation
infect my accent. I am welcomed
in bars and corner-shops, with "It's a soft night."
And yes, I have loved their girls.

See, where fine white clouds drift high above the meadow
the small farm daydreams all doors open:
they are all gone round the bend of the field, out of change.
Behind the clock on the mantel dust thickens on letters
strangely-deciphered, from children "across the water."

From where, too, on my screen come shimmering
images of the old labyrinthine cities,
sanities. Which I can revisit, resume
undetected; noticing how they find
bestial or glamorous our banalities,

and do not see the detail beneath stark outlines.
I am no longer sure that I wish to return,
even though it is winter here now, the sky and land
seeping greyly together. Unsettled, defined
by difference, I find I can live with this,

am strangely involved in, call it, a climate.
Yes, as the mad wind rises, sets the sea
resonating, whips waves white, and plucks
tiles from thin roofs, above which gulls
weave lamentation's dissonant vocables.

ANDREW WATERMAN

GRANDMOTHER

In a house in Fresno, the television
lives with the family like a grandmother from the father's side.
She is up with the wife at six, when the baby daughter cries:
a grandmother willing to help, awake, but silent:
what she thinks flickers across her face without a sound.
While the father sleeps, the mother sits with the grandmother
feeding the baby: the eyes of the wife lift above the spoon
from the face of the child to the face of the silent grandmother.
The day outside begins to fill
with the sun of palmtrees; birds
call again and again from the high branches and leaves.

When the older child gets up, he stands at his doorway in pajamas
to stare at the familiar scene: his mother, grandmother
and the new baby. All day long in his play
in and out of the yard, the house, his meals and the steady sun
he goes back and forth by his grandmother
as she talks to herself, inwardly, her thoughts visible
but noiseless. In the afternoon, when the father wakes
the grandmother speaks to the older child for a while.
The parents glance toward her themselves now and then
as if to hear what she says. And once in the warm evening
the telephone says that the maternal grandmother
across the city is watching something on her own television
she thinks the child might like. All eyes
go on the grandmother, who begins talking again at once.
But the young body loses patience with the old
and she is left to address the empty California air.

Late at night, when the baby and the child are in bed
the parents gratefully turn to the grandmother.
When the mother goes on into the bedroom
the father listens to grandmother alone.
Then she is quiet, while he has his music

but her thoughts still pass restlessly across her face. At last
in the very early morning, the father says goodnight to the
    grandmother
and goes in himself to sleep. The grandmother sleeps,
the father sleeps, the mother sleeps, the little boy sleeps.
The baby turns fretfully in her crib, and cries out.
But there is no answer, and she sinks again, sighing,
back to her warm and milky infant's dream.

                                            TOM WAYMAN

*WHY GOD PERMITS EVIL
FOR ANSWER TO THIS QUESTION
OF INTEREST TO MANY
WRITE BIBLE ANSWERS DEPT. E–7*

—*ad on a matchbook cover*

Of interest to John Calvin and Thomas Aquinas
for instance and Job for instance who never got

one straight answer but only his cattle back.
With interest, which is something, but certainly not

any kind of answer unless you ask
God if God can demonstrate God's power

and God's glory, which is not a question.
You should all be living at this hour.

You had Servetus to burn, the elect to count,
bad eyes and the Institutes to write;

you had the exercises and had Latin,
the hard bunk and the solitary night;

you had the neighbors to listen to and your woman
yelling at you to curse God and die.

Some of this to be on the right side;
some of it to ask in passing, Why?

Why badness makes its way in a world He made?
How come He looked for twelve and got eleven?

You had the faith and looked for love, stood pain,
learned patience and little else. We have E–7.

Churches may be shut down everywhere,
half-written philosophy books be tossed away.

Some place on the south side of Chicago
a lady with wrinkled hose and a small gray

bun of hair sits straight with her knees together
behind a teacher's desk on the third floor

Of an old shirt factory, bankrupt and abandoned
except for this just cause, and on the door:

Dept. E–7. She opens the letters
asking why God permits it and sends a brown

plain envelope to each return address.
But she is not alone. All up and down

the thin and creaking corridors are doors
and desks behind them: E–6, E–5, 4, 3.

A desk for every question, for how we rise
blown up and burned, for how the will is free,

for when is Armageddon, for whether dogs
have souls or not and on and on. On

beyond the alphabet and possible numbers
where cross-legged, naked and alone,

there sits a pale, tall and long-haired woman
upon a cushion of fleece and eiderdown

holding in one hand a hand-written answer,
holding in the other hand a brown

plain envelope. On either side, cobwebbed
and empty baskets sitting on the floor

say *in* and *out*. There is no sound in the room.
There is no knob on the door. Or there is no door.

MILLER WILLIAMS

A PRIVATE SPACE

for Stephanie Sugioka

This is the space where
the question of beauty enters,
in soft slippers, decorous, even a little
obsequious, muted
as if by choice. She kneels with
her pot of steaming tea; as she pours,
the long black screen of hair
falls across her face.
She handles her limbs
as if they were porcelain. She is almost
perfect, except for the space,
the shadowed gap,
in her huge kimono sleeves.
A hint of silver flashes
in that dark, a sliver of moon
on a night in September, the silk
chrysanthemums nodding
like conspirators along the hem
of sky.

(The icon painters of a thousand years
ago, always left
a little space unfinished
somewhere in the work. It was the place,
they said, inviting to the soul—
the place where
the singular could enter the design,
the ultimate intensity of a slight
intrusion.)

One silver stroke: her eyes opened wide
as ivory fans at the flick of a wrist.
The moon slid through the silk
wrappings of the clouds. Later
she would pass through the rooms,
through the lines of mourners, like light

through the elegant
black lacquered slats of blinds, slender
and bright
beyond suspicion.

ELEANOR WILNER

KNOWING THE ENEMY

The sun strikes the whale's back;
he dives, until the sun is overcast
with tons of green. He knows himself
full-grown; the burden that he carried
in his belly like a stone, is gone:
he has given his Jonah back to God.

For years he carried him, under
the furrowed trenches of his brow
and felt him walk by day the caves
under the great hill of his back—
this memory, this earth-bound being
he had been. Since he was small

this manthing had been tangled in
the mangroves of his mind; burning
like swampfire, or the hated sun,
searing him who needed filtered light,
for whom the mist was heaven.
Such preferences are fate.

When, with a great heave, he disgorged
this image that distended him,
he found it strange
how puny his antagonist had grown—
a twin-tailed tadpole
flashing off in foam.

His silver geyser rises in the air;
the bad dreams disappear
like islands off his starboard flank.
He moves, huge, through his own mist,
oiled silver by the moon, arrowed
as St. Sebastian, bristling harpoons.

Eleanor Wilner